WELCOME TO
ULTIMATE GUIDE
TO ROBLOX!

With more than 40 million games available to play, Roblox offers users a whole world of opportunity and fun. Whether you're a fan of RPGs, building games or life sims, prefer going solo or playing with friends, you're sure to find something you love. In this bookazine we'll bring you the very best of Roblox – from essential tips, tricks and secrets for the platform's most popular games to 50 awesome things to do in Roblox, how to create your own Roblox game and much more! So what are you waiting for?!

CONTENTS

GETTING STARTED

GAME GUIDES

50 COOL THINGS TO DO IN ROBLOX

P 20

Duel starting in 107...

Neutral
AidenFuture1

TOP 10s

WELCOME TO ROBLOX!

All you need to know about the online platform that's taking over the gaming world

WHAT IS ROBLOX?

The short answer is that Roblox is a whole world of fun and interaction. With countless games to explore and millions of users online at every moment of the day, there's always something interesting to do. The long answer is found in the thousands of words that make up the publication you're reading right now!

One important thing to understand is that Roblox is not a game, like *Minecraft*, for example, which many Robloxers also enjoy playing. It's also not a metaverse like the one associated with Facebook, or an older version called Second Life that some older readers may remember. Instead, Roblox is a platform where games can be played, with meeting points where players meet and realms that can be explored. For that reason, there's far more to it than just being a game: it's a global community of players, rather like a real-life city where people meet to do various activities, whether solo or in groups.

Continue

🏌 [DUCK CRATE] Tower Defense…
👍 94% 👥 16.4K

Islands 🐾 [HARDCORE…
👍 90% 👥 5.6K

SkyWars 🔥 [BY VOXELS!]
👍 75% 👥 1.3K

Recommended For You

There are over 40 million games to play on Roblox!

...tball

[🐍 Cobra Survive] Rider World
👍 95% 👥 230

Rogue Lineage
👍 84% 👥 245

WHERE DID ROBLOX COME FROM?

Here's a very quick history of Roblox: it was created in 2004 by two developers called David Baszucki and Erik Cassel, who called it DynaBlocks. The game soon adopted its new name – a cross between 'robots' and 'blocks' – and launched on the web in 2006, with the in-game currency system Robux implemented seven years later.

By 2014 it was playable as a mobile phone app on iOS and Android, and the following year a new graphics engine called Smooth Terrain was introduced, making the physics less blocky and much smoother. In subsequent years, Roblox was launched on Xbox and Oculus Rift, and by 2019 there was a membership option called Roblox Premium. As we write these words, you can play Roblox pretty much anywhere as long as you have an internet connection.

The platform is owned by Roblox Corporation, a company based in San Mateo, California, that is still run by David Baszucki: the company is worth over 2 billion real-world dollars. That's a lot of Robux…

FAST FACT

Noobs will often describe Roblox as a game. Nope! It's an 'online game platform and game creation system'.

Roblox is available on almost every platform, from mobiles to consoles and PCs

WHAT CAN I DO IN ROBLOX?

Again, that's what this whole magazine is about, but if you want a quick summary, we'll let you have one right here! On Roblox you can (deep breath): play games, create games, learn scripting language, buy and sell items, meet friends, connect with new people, exchange text and voice messages, join communities of people with similar interests, play exotic roles, solve problems, create art, study academic subjects, interact with famous brands, enter competitions, win prizes, collect rare artefacts, and, most importantly, have a lot of fun!

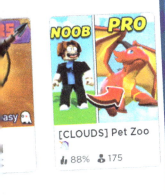

[CLOUDS] Pet Zoo

88% 175

Welcome to Bloxburg

88% 14.2K

There are a whole host of things for you to do in Roblox

WHO'S PLAYING ROBLOX?

Over 50 million active users every single day, that's who! Most of these players are aged between seven and 15, but the 17 to 24-year-old age group is the fastest-growing demographic – those kids may have become adults in recent years, but they're clearly not feeling any pressure to quit using Roblox. This explains why the games on Roblox – reportedly around 40 million of them – have matured in nature a little over the years, with quite a few of them unsuitable for young children (see our 'Staying Safe' guide for more on this).

What's more, the user base is spread pretty much evenly around the world. As an American developed and owned platform, in the early days most Roblox users were in the USA and Canada. This has shifted in recent years, most notably during the recent pandemic, when user numbers leapt by 40 per cent worldwide: nowadays there are more European than American users, and a huge number of players are based in Asia.

Interested in which celebs play Roblox games? There are quite a few, although some of them may be simply present for marketing reasons rather than actively playing games, so don't believe everything you read.

Famous people who we know definitely show up to play – because they've said so in interviews – include the actors Noah Schnapp and Millie Bobby Brown, who play the parts of Will Byers and Eleven in *Stranger Things*. The electronic music duo The Chainsmokers have also talked fondly about their Roblox use, as has the actor Aidan Gallagher of Nickelodeon's *Nicky, Ricky, Dicky & Dawn* series. The social media influencer Charli D'Amelio can be found in the Roblox universe under the nickname @chardunkin1, and the YouTuber Mr Beast hangs out there under the handle @Jimmy_MBG.

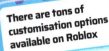
There are tons of customisation options available on Roblox

Tragedy
31

Hungry Dino
50

Pizza Worker Hat
50

Black Pigtails
43

Sk10r Boi
70

True Ninja of Brilliant...
30

Even celebs and influencers enjoy hanging out on Roblox

Stage 18/50 (36%)

FAST FACT

In 2020, Roblox had over 164 million active users every month. This included more than half of all American children under the age of 16.

Skip Stage

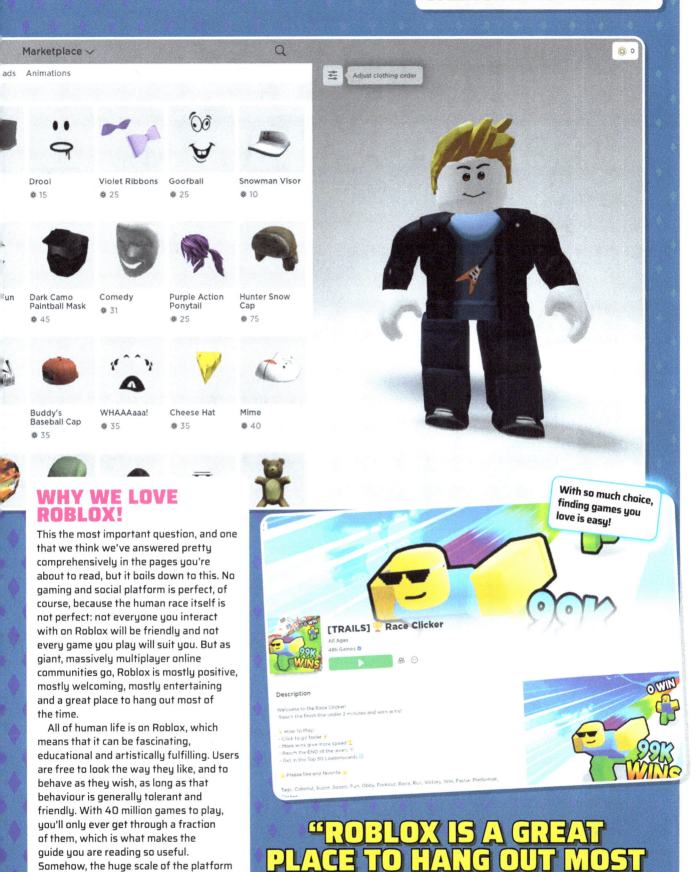

Marketplace ⌄

ads Animations

Drool ◉ 15	Violet Ribbons ◉ 25	Goofball ◉ 25	Snowman Visor ◉ 10
Dark Camo Paintball Mask ◉ 45	Comedy ◉ 31	Purple Action Ponytail ◉ 25	Hunter Snow Cap ◉ 75
Buddy's Baseball Cap ◉ 35	WHAAAaaa! ◉ 35	Cheese Hat ◉ 35	Mime ◉ 40

Adjust clothing order

With so much choice, finding games you love is easy!

[TRAILS] 🏆 Race Clicker
All Ages
48h Games ☑

Description

Welcome to the Race Clicker!
Reach the finish line under 2 minutes and earn wins!

🏁 How To Play:
- Click to go faster ⚡
- More wins give more speed 🏆
- Reach the END of the levels 🏁
- Get in the Top 50 Leaderboards 🏅

💖 Please like and favorite 💖

Tags: Colorful, Super, Speed, Fun, Obby, Parkour, Race, Run, Victory, Win, Faster, Platformer, Clicker

0 WIN
99K WINS

WHY WE LOVE ROBLOX!

This the most important question, and one that we think we've answered pretty comprehensively in the pages you're about to read, but it boils down to this. No gaming and social platform is perfect, of course, because the human race itself is not perfect: not everyone you interact with on Roblox will be friendly and not every game you play will suit you. But as giant, massively multiplayer online communities go, Roblox is mostly positive, mostly welcoming, mostly entertaining and a great place to hang out most of the time.

All of human life is on Roblox, which means that it can be fascinating, educational and artistically fulfilling. Users are free to look the way they like, and to behave as they wish, as long as that behaviour is generally tolerant and friendly. With 40 million games to play, you'll only ever get through a fraction of them, which is what makes the guide you are reading so useful. Somehow, the huge scale of the platform is what makes it so appealing – you never know what each new visit to Roblox will hold.

With all that in mind, welcome to Roblox – and we'll see you there!

"ROBLOX IS A GREAT PLACE TO HANG OUT MOST OF THE TIME"

ROBLOX: A NEED TO KNOW GUIDE

Your essential guide to getting started on Roblox

The sheer numbers attached to Roblox – 40 million games, billions of visits, thousands of microtransactions a minute – make it seem a bit intimidating, don't they? But never fear: this fun-packed platform is actually a piece of cake to download, operate and explore. If you're new to Roblox – and hey, we all were once – then read this easy-to-grasp guide to getting started. We'll see you there!

Recommended For You

There are lots of different types of games to play

🏈 Ultimate Football
📶 89% 👤 2.3K

Welcome to Bloxburg
📶 88% 👤 13.6K

[🧡JELLY] Pet Simulator X! 🐾
📶 92% 👤 74.7K

Deepwoken: Verse 2
📶 89% 👤 4.2K

Rogue Lineage
📶 84% 👤 304

The Wild W
📶 88% 👤 1

Royale High

Catalog Avatar Creator

Emergency Response: Liberty...

[PIRATE ISLAND] Fishing...

Wisteria 2 [ALPHA]

REx: Reinca

HOW TO FIND AND DOWNLOAD ROBLOX

Choose a device. You can play Roblox on a PC or Mac computer, an Apple or Android phone, or on an Xbox One, Series X or Series S console. Whichever one you choose, open up a web browser and head to www.roblox.com, where you'll find the download you need. Note that other websites offer this service, but stay away from them because they're unofficial and therefore unsafe. If you're under 13 or not quite sure what to do here, ask a parent or guardian to help.

The first thing to do at the Roblox homepage is to click on a game – it doesn't matter which one, as long as it's age-appropriate. Click the green button with the Play icon: this triggers the download of the Roblox platform to your device, either at the Play Store and App Store on your phone or with a file called RobloxPlayerLauncher.exe on your computer, which you'll need to unpack and run. On Xbox, install it via the Xbox Store. Again, ask for help if you're unsure how this step works.

Once Roblox is installed on your device, it may need to be updated to the current version. Most devices will take care of this automatically or simply ask for permission to update. Simply follow the instructions, and you're ready to create your account.

FAST FACT

Roblox is free to use: you don't need to spend any money to have a great time on the platform.

CREATE AN ACCOUNT

This step couldn't be simpler. All you have to do is enter your date of birth, username and password. You'll need a parent or guardian's permission before setting up an account, and an active email address so Roblox can confirm your details.

The platform doesn't have a minimum age for anyone who just wants to play the games, but it does require players to be aged at least 13 to access the social media and messaging features, so to stay safe, make sure you enter your real date of birth. Don't be tempted to state that you're older than your real age. If you're a parent or guardian who is setting up an account for a child, you may wish to turn on the parental controls: see our 'Staying Safe' guide for more on this subject.

Project Flight | Early Access...
👍 94% 👤 217

[ANNIVERSARY] Mighty Omega
👍 87% 👤 1.1K

PLS DONATE 💸

Football Fusion 2

"IF YOU'RE UNDER 13 OR NOT SURE WHAT TO DO, ASK A PARENT OR GUARDIAN TO HELP"

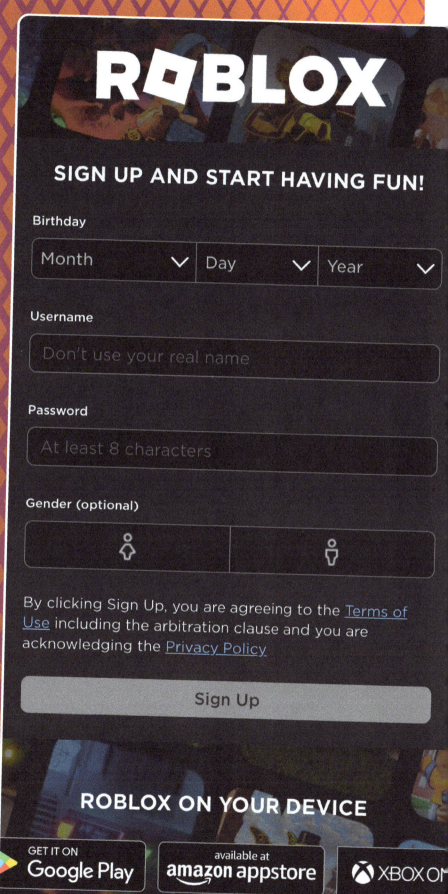

SIGN UP AND START HAVING FUN!

Birthday

| Month ⌄ | Day ⌄ | Year ⌄ |

Username

Don't use your real name

Password

At least 8 characters

Gender (optional)

By clicking Sign Up, you are agreeing to the Terms of Use including the arbitration clause and you are acknowledging the Privacy Policy

Sign Up

ROBLOX ON YOUR DEVICE

GET IT ON Google Play

available at amazon appstore

XBOX ON

CHOOSE A USERNAME WISELY

While you're setting up your account as above, you'll need to choose a username and a display name: the first one is your login and is unique to you, and the second is the one everyone sees in-game. You'd think that choosing these names would be easy, right? Well, you'd be surprised how many regret their initial choice of names because they're silly, cheesy or whatever. Funny as it is to choose a name that mentions your favourite pop star, food or animal, you may decide to go back later on and change it, especially if you made a spelling mistake when you typed it into the box. Hey, we've all been there.

You can easily change your display name once every seven days, but changing your username is a little more complex and definitely more expensive. To do this, select the Settings cog at the top right of your screen, go to the Account Info tab, click the pencil icon and make the edit. You'll then have to pay 1,000 Robux (ouch!) to complete the change. Note that other players can still see your previous usernames, so this isn't a useful strategy if you're trying to hide from another player.

Once you're all set, you're ready to create and customise your avatar – the character you control in-game. We have a whole section coming up devoted to ways to make a cool avatar, so let's just say here that after you finish setting up your account, you'll be taken to a home page where you can choose the look and clothes that you want. Then it's game on!

> Use the search option or try one of the suggested games to get started

> There are lots of free customisation options, but you have to pay for others

Gang O' Fries ⊙ 250

You May Also Like

Cheeks ⊙ 75

Narrow ⊙ 75

Strong Jaw ⊙ 100

Paragon ⊙ 250

Chiseled ⊙ 300

Shop for More

FAST FACT

Premium Membership is currently £9.99 per month, which gets you 1,000 Robux 12 times a year. However, you don't need Premium Membership to have a good time on Roblox!

> You can customise everything from your avatar's appearance to their clothes and accessories

Fighters Simulator

erful enemies and become strong in this epic sword

FIND AND PLAY GAMES

As soon as you load Roblox on your device, a range of games will be suggested for you, but you can use the search bar to find more. Simply click on any one you like, then click Play, and it will load immediately. Use the Menu button in the top left-hand corner of your screen for in-game options. It's worth spending a minute learning what your choices are.

Move your avatar around the game with your keyboard, using the letter keys WASD to move forward, back and sideways, or simply use the arrow keys. The space bar allows you to jump, and you can climb a ladder simply by walking towards it.

The camera position – in other words, the angle from which you view your avatar – is controlled with the right mouse button. You can also turn it left or right using the < and > keys or the left and right arrow keys.

If you prefer, you can choose between Classic and Follow modes: the first of these keeps the camera fixed in one spot until you move it, while the second tracks you from left to right as you move.

You'll also notice that you have clickable Move, Copy and Delete tools: these allow you to interact with various in-game objects. The Move tool moves an item around, the Copy tool will make a copy of it, and the Delete tool will make it vanish. As you collect items, they'll be automatically stored in your backpack: this includes anything from tools, power-ups and musical instruments to weapons. Check what's in your pack and organise its contents by clicking or tapping the backpack button in the upper left corner of your screen.

Finally, when you want to quit out, click Leave Game on the menu. A window will ask you to confirm, and you'll be on your merry way.

INTERACTING WITH OTHER PLAYERS

Bearing in mind the rules about safety on Roblox that we talk about in the 'Staying Safe' section, you can chat with, trade with and become online friends with all sorts of cool people while playing games or just hanging out at gathering places. To talk to someone, walk up to them and press the / key: a chat window will open up and you can say hi. Not all games allow this, however.

Becoming friends with other players is easy, too. If you know someone's username, search for them in the search box, selecting the People category first. Click their profile and you'll be taken to their account page, where you can select Add Friend. If you don't know the person already, Roblox recommends that you send a short, polite message explaining who you are and where you met them, for example 'Hi, I'm Mike – we played Meep City together earlier today'.

If the person doesn't accept your friend request, don't worry about it. Maybe they rarely visit Roblox and don't want to build a friends list. Likewise, you don't have to accept any friend requests either.

To trade items with a player, you'll need a Premium membership. Think carefully before buying one of these, as Roblox is perfectly playable without it. If you do take the plunge though, you can trade with someone by opening their profile, clicking the three dots at the upper right corner and then clicking Trade Items.

Select the item you want to trade, which is then added to the Your Offers list, and select the item that you want from the other player, which will appear on the Your Requests list. Click Make Offer, and then it's down to the other person to accept or decline. Check your messages for progress. If you're including Robux in your offer, remember that a transaction fee of 30 per cent will be automatically deducted from it.

Where do I get Robux, we hear you say? Read on...

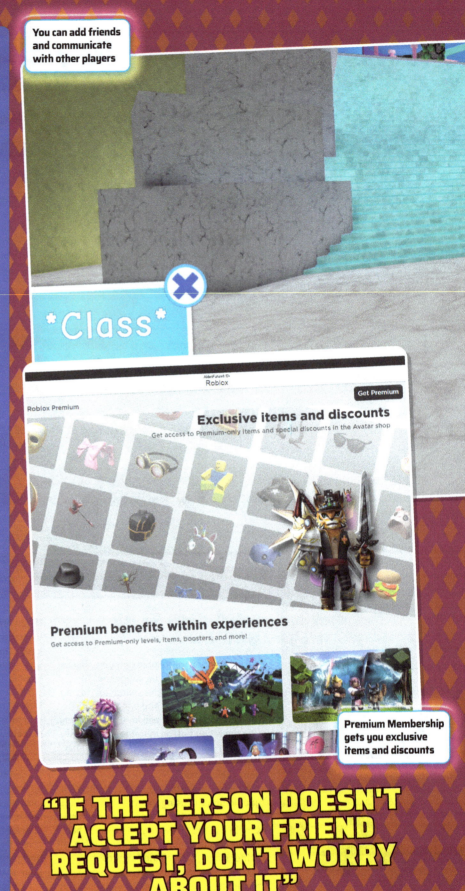

You can add friends and communicate with other players

Class

Premium Membership gets you exclusive items and discounts

"IF THE PERSON DOESN'T ACCEPT YOUR FRIEND REQUEST, DON'T WORRY ABOUT IT"

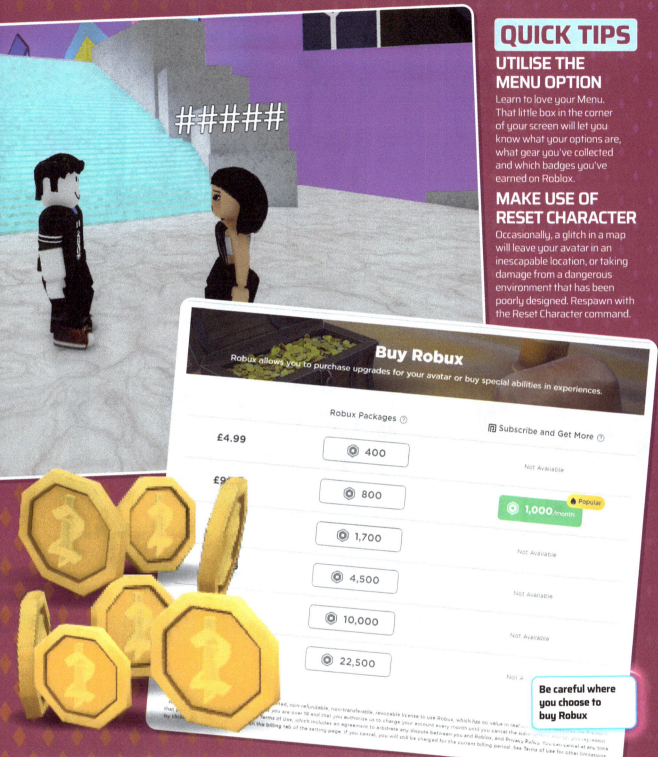

QUICK TIPS

UTILISE THE MENU OPTION

Learn to love your Menu. That little box in the corner of your screen will let you know what your options are, what gear you've collected and which badges you've earned on Roblox.

MAKE USE OF RESET CHARACTER

Occasionally, a glitch in a map will leave your avatar in an inescapable location, or taking damage from a dangerous environment that has been poorly designed. Respawn with the Reset Character command.

Buy Robux

Robux allows you to purchase upgrades for your avatar or buy special abilities in experiences.

Robux Packages ⑦		Subscribe and Get More ⑦
£4.99	◉ 400	Not Available
£9	◉ 800	◉ 1,000/month ● Popular
	◉ 1,700	Not Available
	◉ 4,500	Not Available
	◉ 10,000	Not Available
	◉ 22,500	Not A...

Be careful where you choose to buy Robux

ROBUX EXPLAINED

Like money in real life, Robux is a currency within Roblox that can be earned, saved, donated or spent. Whatever you want to buy in Roblox, you can buy with this useful currency – but also like in real life, it doesn't come for free. You'll need to earn it by working a job in Roblox, in which case you're giving up time that you could be using to do real-world activities such as hanging out with friends, or you can buy Robux with real-life money that you could spend on loads of other stuff. So be warned!

Safety is paramount here because actual real-life money is at risk. Never trust anyone who offers you free Robux. Don't bother with websites or apps that call themselves 'Robux Generators' or similar: they may steal your bank details and get you banned from the game. If you really want some Robux, try buying some with a small amount of real money – and we do mean a small amount, after getting the permission of a parent or guardian – to get you started.

Now that you have a Roblox account, a cool username and Robux in the bank, let's get your avatar looking fresh!

QUICK TIPS

BE A FASHION MOGUL

Did you know that you can design and sell avatar clothes at the Catalog? You can find the templates online, and it's easy to create them. Upload them to the store for 10 Robux, pay another 10 when they sell, and finally, hand over another 30 per cent of the fee paid by the buyer.

R YOU READY?

If you can, play with a six-limbed (R6) and 15-limbed (R15) avatar in various experiences. Not only do they move differently and give you a wider experience of Roblox; they attract quite different friends – traditionalists and more progressive players.

CREATING YOUR AVATAR

Be the coolest-looking player in the whole of Roblox!

WHAT IS AN AVATAR, ANYWAY?

Simply put, it's you! Your avatar is the character you control – the little person who runs around the game map, collects stuff and completes tasks. You can use the Menu in the top corner of the screen to see how much gear your avatar is carrying, and there are on-screen counters in many games to tell you about its mood, health and much more. Once you launch Roblox, click on the Avatar icon and you'll find yourself at the Avatar Editor screen. Here, you'll be able to customise your little adventurer's clothing, accessories, body and animations. These are great fun, but if you want to do even more customising, you need to step up your game to the next level...

You can customise your avatar however you want

Got a style in mind? You should be able to replicate it

HOW DO I CUSTOMISE MY AVATAR IN ROBLOX STUDIO?

Roblox Studio is the creative arm of Roblox, and is where you'll create games – see our dedicated section on that very subject – but it's also able to customise the appearance, behaviour and performance of your avatar. You'll probably enter the Studio with your avatar settings determined to an extent by the actions you performed at the Avatar Editor screen, but if you want to tweak them further, you can do that here.

The bit of code you will need is 'HumanoidDescription'. Using this deceptively simple term, you can do various things to beef up your avatar. Within that description, you can begin by choosing whether your character has six or 15 limbs, 'limbs' meaning any individual body part, not just arms and legs. You can access a wider or narrower set of animations, and amend the collision boundaries for the characters within a given experience – either fixed or dynamic. You can even edit the Asset IDs – or properties – of your avatar's height, width and other dimensions, clothing, body parts and body colours. It's like Dr Frankenstein's laboratory, but harmless.

HOW CAN I USE ROBLOX STUDIO TO DESIGN MY CLOTHES?

With the greatest of ease! Start with a T-shirt, the easiest garment to make. Create an image sized 512 x 512 pixels and upload it via the Asset Manager. A T-shirt is just a square decal, so that's it. If you fancy something more ambitious, find Roblox's templates for work shirts and trousers ('pants' to our transatlantic friends) and wrap your designs around them. There's a size guide that you'll need to stick to, or the upload will fail.

Make your avatar more distinctive in Roblox Studio

CAN I BUY STUFF FOR MY AVATAR?

Of course you can, assuming you've got enough in-game cash. Head to the Avatar Shop, which players often refer to as the Catalog (note the American spelling), and you'll encounter a vast number of player- and game-created merchandise for your avatar to wear. When we say vast, we mean astoundingly, ridiculously huge: when we sorted the contents of the Catalog with free stuff first, it took us ten scrolls just to get through the free hairstyles. Flip the order the other way, and you'll see gear that costs millions of Robux, causing our bank manager to fall off his chair.

I'M BROKE. WHAT FREEBIES CAN I GET?

Lacking Robux? Never fear – there are often Roblox promo codes to be found that allow you to get free gear for your avatar. They tend to be time-limited, though, so you'll need to move quickly. Like we said, though, even without codes or Bux, you'll find tons of free gear in the Avatar Shop. There's pretty much no need to pay for anything, if you ask us. Simply click Get Now on the freebie you like and it will be added to your inventory as quick as a flash. Keep coming back regularly to see what else is available at the cost of no more than a couple of clicks!

You can even design your avatar's clothes in Roblox

TOP 10 TIPS FOR STAYING SAFE ON ROBLOX

Follow these essential tips for a safe and friendly experience on Roblox

DON'T SHARE PERSONAL INFORMATION

1 Most Robloxers are perfectly honest, just as most people are in real life, but you can't tell from a display name and an avatar if a player is trustworthy or not. For this reason, never share your real name, address or personal and financial details with anyone, even if you've been playing with them for some time. It's just not worth the risk.

PLAY AGE-APPROPRIATE GAMES

2 Roblox rates its games as All Ages, 9+ and 13+, with the main difference being the amount and realism of any avatar blood spilled in combat. Players and parents should be aware of these ratings, and that a small amount of content is graphic and against Roblox's rules, despite moderators' efforts to remove it.

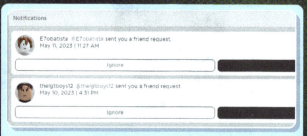

ONLY ADD PEOPLE YOU KNOW AS FRIENDS

4 A good tip is to keep your Roblox friends list restricted to people that you actually know in real life. That way, conversations will generally be more friendly than they would be between randoms who don't know each other. You can still play with people that you don't know without adding them as friends – Roblox enables friendly interactions between strangers, after all.

BE HONEST ABOUT YOUR AGE

3 We know how tempting it is to add a couple of years to your real age when Roblox asks you to enter your date of birth, but it does this for good reason. A whole stack of laws govern Roblox's operations in many different countries, designed to protect players who are not yet adults. These can't protect you as effectively if you're untruthful about your real age.

FAST FACT

Block any user from messaging you in the three-dot menu on their profile page. You can do this in-game or at the Roblox homepage.

PLAY ROBLOX AS A FAMILY

5 There's no better way to explore a fun game than playing it together, so why not schedule time for kids and parents/guardians to embark on a campaign as a family? That way, everyone can solve problems together and keep an eye out for any possible issues as a team.

USE SAFETY SETTINGS

6 Parental controls can be applied in Settings (click the cog icon), where parents or guardians can disable chat or messaging, restrict access to certain games and set a monthly limit on how many Robux, if any, the player is allowed to spend. Parents, explain clearly to your child why you're doing this – they'll understand that it's for their benefit.

DON'T FALL FOR SCAMS

7 The rule is that if something looks too good to be true, it probably is. Most Roblox players won't try to steal your money, but a small number of wrongdoers may attempt to take your goods without payment during a trade deal, or try to convince you to send them Robux for various reasons. Don't entertain any such offers.

BLOCK AND REPORT

8 The blocking and reporting functions are in Roblox for a reason. You probably don't need to block every single person who slightly annoys you, but in cases where a fellow player is offensively rude or behaves in a way that contravenes Roblox regulations, a warning followed by a block and report is probably a wise course of action.

TALK TO YOUR PARENTS

9 Communication is everything. If someone is unpleasant to you on Roblox, or says something to you that raises any kind of red flag, tell your parents or guardian. They may not be familiar with the world of online gaming, so you may have to explain the situation in basic terms, but once they understand the problem they'll be able to help you solve it.

TAKE A BREAK

10 Surround yourself with good people in Roblox. If anyone is less than friendly, don't chat with them. If they're annoying, block them. If you still find that the platform is stressful or just not as much fun as you were hoping, why not take a break from Roblox for a month or two? When you come back, there will be new games to play and just as many cool people to hang out with.

QUICK TIPS

CHECK SAFE GUIDANCE

There are several reliable guides online that will help you make the most of your gaming experience. A good example is Childline's Staying Safe Online page at www.childline.org.uk.

DON'T FEED THE TROLLS

Most Roblox players just want to have fun and enjoy themselves. Rude, selfish or aggressive Robloxers are very much in the minority, but if you do encounter unpleasant messages or behaviour, don't engage with them. Simply block them and move on.

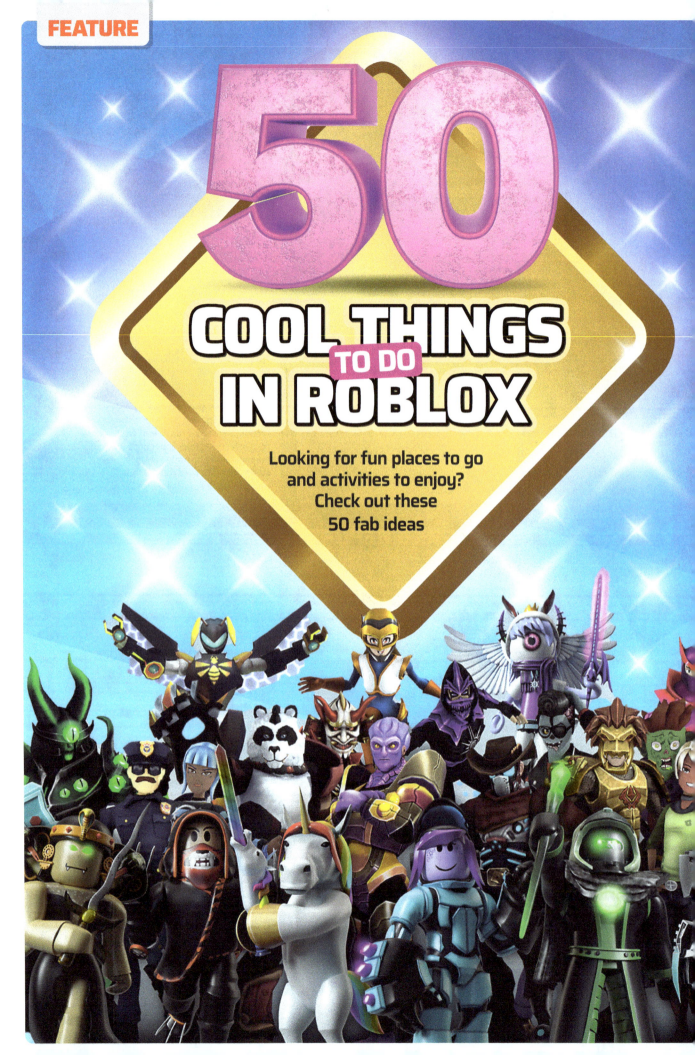

50

COOL THINGS TO DO IN ROBLOX

Looking for fun places to go
and activities to enjoy?
Check out these
50 fab ideas

SEARCH FOR TREASURE BENEATH THE SEA

1 You can have fun for hours in this game! Use your Robux to buy all the gear you need to explore under the sea, hunt for treasure and bring all the items you find back to the surface. Sell them on for power-ups that will help you explore even more, but you need to make sure you get back to the surface for some air, or it'll be game over.

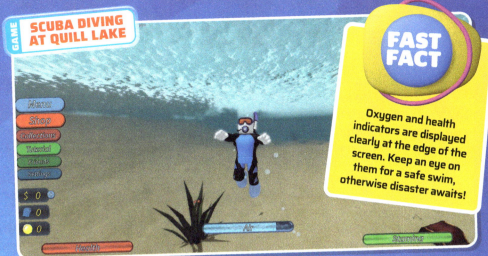

GAME SCUBA DIVING AT QUILL LAKE

FAST FACT

Oxygen and health indicators are displayed clearly at the edge of the screen. Keep an eye on them for a safe swim, otherwise disaster awaits!

GAME ADOPT ME!

RAISE A BABY MONSTER

2 Head to a pet shop, buy an egg and wait until it hatches, at which point your job is to make sure that your little pet grows up safe and happy. You don't know exactly which creature you're going to get, so be prepared. Trade goods with other pet owners and give presents to your little buddy!

GAME WORK AT A PIZZA PLACE

MAKE A PIZZA

3 Here's a fun simulation of what's it's like to earn a living as a pizza maker. Just follow the instructions, gather the ingredients, bake your yummy snack, hop in the car and make deliveries. You'll get a bunch of Robux for doing this, so why not buy your own pizza parlour?

You are now

Pizza Boxer

ADVENTURE AT THE SOUTH POLE

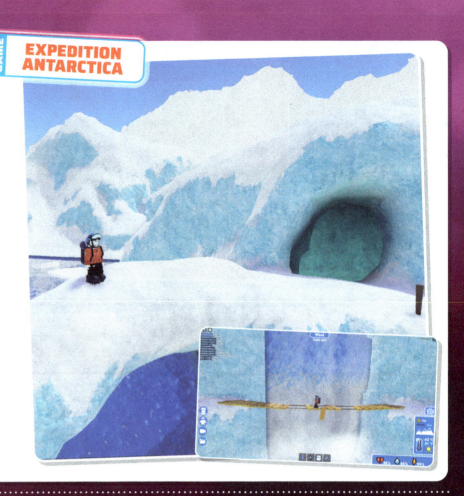

EXPEDITION ANTARCTICA

4 Take care as you set off on this snowy adventure with your team-mates, because when you leave base camp, you'll need to fight through blizzards and deep snow to the Antarctic pole. You'll have a map to help you, though, and you can use Robux to get the essential gear you'll need for the journey. There will be lots to see, of course, but just as much to be careful of along the way – namely polar bears, avalanches and even the odd killer whale or two!

SLAP PEOPLE SILLY

5 Run around the map equipped with a massive hand to slap your enemies! Yes, it's as nuts as it sounds, but the fun doesn't stop there. You'll level up your superpowers as you go, so not only can you slap other players, you can shoot them, blow them up and more. There are loads of levels and places to explore, too.

GAME **SLAP BATTLES**

wolti2099

GAME **ISLAND ROYALE!**

BE THE LAST ONE STANDING

6 In this game, you're thrown into a tropical island environment, where you need to make friends and watch out for enemies as you try to survive. It's a full-on battle here, so keep your wits about you, form alliances, gather resources and level up as you strive to be the last Robloxer standing.

HAVE A SHOOT-OUT

7 Here's a straight-up shooting game in which you get to use all kinds of weapons to take out other players. It's super fast, though; you'll have to dodge bullets while jumping from roof to roof and diving for cover. Make sure you work as part of a team and use every trick available – it's not just about guns in this campaign.

GAME ARSENAL

FAST FACT

If your mobile-phone thumb speed isn't up to scratch, try playing Arsenal on a computer instead. Your reaction time may be the difference between success and failure.

BUILD A THEME PARK

8 As you can read elsewhere, in this game you start out with a piece of land where you can build up your very own theme park from scratch. You'll need to include all the obvious attractions, such as rollercoasters and rides. There's also a leaderboard where you can see how well your park is doing against other players, so there's a bit of competition to keep you on your toes!

GAME THEME PARK TYCOON 2

SURVIVE A NATURAL DISASTER

10 In this game, your friendly avatar has wound up in a sticky situation: a natural disaster has taken place, and the goal is to survive at all costs. This usually requires getting the heck out of the way of falling debris that is designed to kill you. Sometimes, the simpler the game, the more addictive it is.

PLAY CARDS WITH YOUR BUDDIES

9 Remember the card game, UNO? Well, this is a similar game in the world of Roblox, where you can play with your friends or randoms. If you get bored of the standard game, try out the teams mode where you play cooperatively alongside friends to take on groups of other players. It adds a fun twist to the game.

GAME LOCOFFICIAL

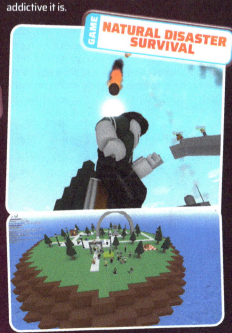

GAME NATURAL DISASTER SURVIVAL

ESCAPE FROM JAIL

11 This game is a basic 'get out of jail' runaround in which you and your team need to escape from prison and avoid the attention of the guards. It sounds simple, but even if you make it out, you'll constantly be hunted down by cops, cars, helicopters and drones. You can also choose to play as a police officer if you wish.

GAME **JAILBREAK**

COMPLETE QUESTS!

12 This game has so much cool content that you could be lost for days in the map! The basic object of the campaign is to complete quests, levelling up each time you complete one. Cool storylines make it fun, while buyable items will help you beat the bad guys.

GAME **BLOX FRUITS**

STAR IN A REALITY SHOW

13 This game plays out like an edgy reality show in which you're looking out for number one – and will have to betray friends to survive. It's like *The Hunger Games*, only slightly less messy! There's plenty of strategy involved here, so keep your wits about you and don't get too attached to any other players – they could be out to stab you in the back.

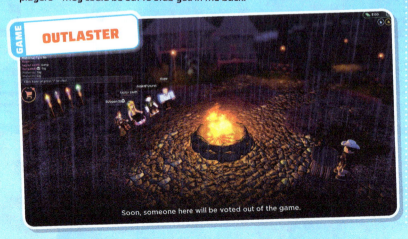

GAME **OUTLASTER**

Soon, someone here will be voted out of the game.

GAME **BEDWARS**

PROTECT YOUR BASE

14 Bedwars, which was inspired by elements of games such as SkyWars, is sure to keep you entertained for hours. Yes, the map can feel a little intimidating when you first enter, but your only objective is to protect your base while attacking enemy bases. Make sure your base doesn't get destroyed, or it's all over!

GAME MALL TYCOON

BUILD A MALL

15 Build your own mall with as many shops as you want on as many as 12 floors. You can also create a custom layout while investing in the features that suit your mall and the shops you build there. Some shops can't be unlocked until you've built up enough money or unearthed the correct code, so there's always more to do!

GAME SPEED RUN 4

RUN LIKE CRAZY

16 The object of this game is simple: run as fast as you possibly can and somersault your way to the finish line. There's a yellow platform at the start to help you rev up your speed before you shoot off, and the end of the line is the end of the map! There are a bunch of levels and environments to enjoy, and a leaderboard will keep track of your speed and progress as you compete against other players.

FAST FACT

All speed runs can be improved by studying the terrain carefully. Check online for other players' tips for a faster performance.

INHABIT A VIRTUAL CITY

17 See the full Bloxburg entry for more details, but for now, let's say that this amazing city simulator allows you to be anyone you want to be and live exactly how you want to live. Decorate your house, go to work, buy items and interact with other players: Bloxburg is so huge that you could get lost in it for hours!

GAME WELCOME TO BLOXBURG

HAVE FUN FIGHTING CRIME

18 This game is a spin-off from the TV anime *Miraculous: Tales Of Ladybug & Cat Noir*. Play as your own avatar, or choose to become one of the characters from the show. As well as fighting crime and embarking on adventures, you'll love the minigames hidden deep within the map.

GAME **MIRACULOUS RP**

LIVETOPIA

GAME

BUILD A NEW LIFE

19 Livetopia is an immersive virtual world where you can do whatever you want in various roles. You can interact with other players, build your own house, get a job, explore the world and simply have fun on the map. It's rather similar to Welcome To Bloxburg, but the graphics are a little slicker.

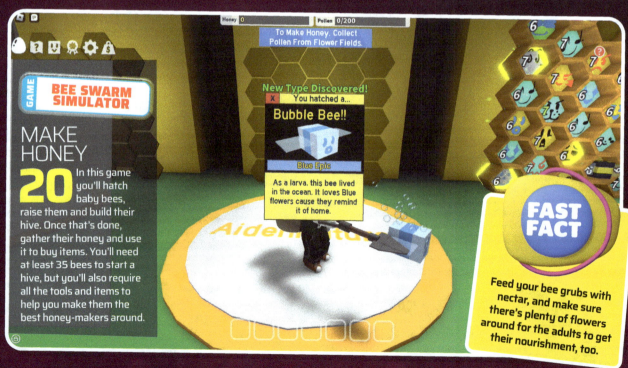

GAME **BEE SWARM SIMULATOR**

MAKE HONEY

20 In this game you'll hatch baby bees, raise them and build their hive. Once that's done, gather their honey and use it to buy items. You'll need at least 35 bees to start a hive, but you'll also require all the tools and items to help you make them the best honey-makers around.

FAST FACT

Feed your bee grubs with nectar, and make sure there's plenty of flowers around for the adults to get their nourishment, too.

HAVE MEGA ADVENTURES

21 This multigame platform allows you to play on a large number of stages: in fact, Mega Easy Obby has over 800 of them to play with, on many levels. The general objective is to jump through obstacles and avoid getting killed, which is harder than it sounds – in fact, getting through all 800 challenges might take months!

GAME
MEGA EASY OBBY

GAME
SONIC SPEED SIMULATOR

BECOME SONIC

22 Everyone's favourite fleet-footed hedgehog is alive and well in Roblox, with a humongous world to explore. All his friends, including the adorable Tails the fox, are here too, so help Sonic defeat the scary Eggman, Dr Robotnik, and blast through this exciting map.

PLAY ULTIMATE HIDE AND SEEK

GAME
HIDE AND SEEK EXTREME

23 We've all played this in real life: one player is chosen as 'It' at the start, before everyone runs and hides. You'll be equipped with items to help you on your mission, if you're chosen as It, which is a relief, because the maps are huge. You play as a tiny version of yourself, jumping over huge obstacles and climbing into crevasses to hide.

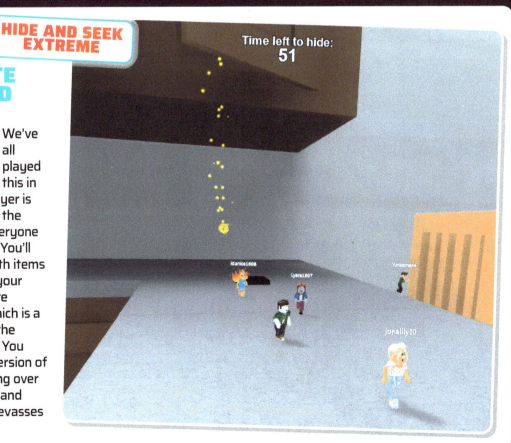

OWN A DRAGON

24 Raise your dragon from an egg to a fully grown monster while designing a base for it. As scary as dragons may be, you'll have to protect your brood as you take to the skies and fly with them. Train them up to become independent, explore different realms and enjoy any number of adventures with your fiery friends.

GAME **DRAGON ADVENTURES**

CHOOSE YOUR DRAGON

Rocirus

Welcome! I'm Rodger, your guide.

Choose a dragon you like, and we can begin!

Choose

CRACK THE PUZZLE

25 In this puzzle game you have to direct laser beams using mirrors, aiming them at an end point called a node. This is essentially a power point that you need to charge with your laser beam, which sounds simple, but becomes complex as the 50 different puzzles unfold. Luckily, there are tutorials along the way to help you.

GAME **MIRROR MUSE**

Puzzle Complete!

Next

Current Perk: None

Oh! You didn't select a perk yet.

< Confirm >

GAME **TWILIGHT DAYCARE**

BE A BIG BABY!

26 Roleplay as a baby in a daycare centre, or choose to play as an adult character in the game. There are tonnes of fun places to explore, and you can choose from a roomful of toys to play with. Check out the bubble room – every house should have one of these, babies or no babies.

LIVE A CRIMINAL LIFE

27 Warning: this shooter game might not be suitable for very young Robloxers, but it'll be plenty of fun for older players. In Notoriety, you'll shoot through various scenarios to level up your arsenal. You're the bad guy here, so fight the police and commit crimes to become rich and powerful.

GAME **NOTORIETY**

GAME **FIELD OF BATTLE**

EXPLORE A FANTASY WORLD

28 In this game, you find yourself playing in a fantasy world full of wizards and monsters. Battle orcs and other bad guys to take control of key locations within the map, buying items to help you level up as you go. There's a huge world to explore, so gather gems and fight the mobs!

Food Limit (0 / 50)

Deposit

BAKE AND MAKE MONEY

29 You're a food tycoon here, investing in simple equipment and starting small as you build up your business. You'll need to buy special equipment and production lines to bake the food that you're selling, but make sure that everything works smoothly in your factory. Accidents will happen – and they will cost you!

GAME **FOOD EMPIRE**

FAST FACT

Invest wisely in any tycoon game. Spend too much at the outset and you risk going broke. Under-invest and your business will never get off the ground!

SCORE: -1580

FUNKY FRIDAY

GAME

By GRANTARE, LANCEY, RUBYSART... AND THE VS DAVE AND BAMBI: GOLDEN APPLE EDITION TEAM
02:07

COMPETE IN A DANCE-OFF

30 This game is a full-on dance competition where you choose the music, setting and level you want to dance to – all while slicing swords through the air. Follow the on-screen arrows to mimic the dance steps and win different awards, but watch out for those flashing blades, for heaven's sake.

FAST FACT

The idea of dancing with swords can be traced back to the Japanese martial art kendo and the Brazilian combat style capoeira. Don't try either at home!

KEEP YOUR HOUSE INTACT

31 What the heck? In this map, houses are stacked on top of each other in a huge tower: your job is to keep your house safe. Evil mobs will try to steal your health, and you and your house could be struck by lightning or encounter some other disaster at any moment. Which evil genius dreamed this one up?

GAME HORRIFIC HOUSING

Customise

GAME ROBLOX STUDIO

BUILD YOUR OWN GAME

32 Check our full story on this, but you can use Roblox Studio to create games from templates or start from scratch. You can also work on building worlds with your friends. There are many available tools to use in your build, and you can customise most of the items to suit your needs. Building your own game and seeing people enjoy it is an incredible experience.

GAME SHARK BITE

DODGE THE SHARK

33 In this game, you'll team up with hunters to escape a marauding shark – unless you want to play as the shark! As a player, buy the boat of your dreams and add armour – if you're the shark, select your species and choose how many teeth you have. The more the merrier, obviously.

FIND GEMS AND JEWELS

GAME · MINING SIMULATOR

34 Go mining for treasures with a team of your friends, or on your own if you don't want to share the loot. Find as many gems as you can, level up and become rich. Acquire pets to help you dig for treasure, and stock up on tools to help you as you explore the mines and caves.

GAME

MINING SIMULATOR

GAME

FREEZE TAG

TAG YOUR FRIENDS

35 This is just like the real game of It: run around trying to tag your friends, or run from whoever is It. If you get caught, you'll be frozen into a block of ice – fortunately, you can buy your way out of it, or ask your friends to rescue you. There will be a few attackers, so keep an eye out!

126

GAME

EPIC MINIGAMES

PARTY TIME!

36 Ready for the ultimate fun map? There are 124 minigames to explore here, as you earn coins and level up your avatar. The map works like a virtual arcade where there's always tonnes to do, with mazes, puzzles, quests and battles – you'll never want to leave! Some lag issues have been reported, but the game mostly works fine, and the fact that you have so much variety here makes it one of the very best things to do in Roblox.

GET ADORABLE PETS

37 In this game, your avatar collects coins in order to collect cute pets. You hatch them from eggs, and then these pets in turn will help you buy more animals as you go. It's a simple task, but always an enjoyable one, especially when you watch your little furry friends follow you about as you go on adventures. You can trade your pets with other players, upgrade them, and even fuse your pets together to make even better ones. Train them, hang out with other trainers, and remember that there are different levels to unlock.

OWN A CAT CAFÉ

38 In this roleplaying game, you'll run your very own Hello Kitty-themed café. The great thing about this RPG is that you can join up with your friends and run it together. You'll start with a simple coffee truck, but as your business grows you can upgrade to a fully equipped café with employees and customers.

PLAY PAINTBALL

39 Choose from a range of weapons and take part in this super-fast paintball game, as you team up with buddies and battle it out against a common enemy. There are lots of places to explore and levels to reach, and as you progress you will be able to get your hands on bigger and better guns.

SURVIVE A DESERT ISLAND

40 This is a survival game on a desert island where you need to gather food and supplies to live in the wild. You can team up with other players to help you survive as you explore this huge map, and you'll need to build useful items such as clothes, rafts and weapons. The winner is the most successful survivor.

GAME: BOOGA BOOGA REBORN!

GET ARTY

41 In this game we play alongside our buddies, drawing pictures and asking other players to guess what we're working on. An artist is chosen in each round to draw a word, and if you guess correctly then you'll win points that you can use to buy items in the game. It's a bit like Pictionary, but with no need for paper and pens!

GAME: DRAW IT!

SOLVE THE CRIME

42 The object here is to escape a murderer and solve his or her crime. You can be anyone in the game: the innocents, the police officer or the murderer. The cop is the only one with a gun, and therefore the only player who can stop the murderer – if that's you, be secret about it or else the killer will target you!

GAME: MURDER MYSTERY 2

LIVE AN ISLAND LIFE

43 This huge game provides you with much to learn as you progress, but master its secrets and it'll keep you involved for many hours. The map is made up of floating islands in the sky, where you can build structures, collect items and take part in quests. It's a whole world of combat, work, trading, pet care and more.

GAME: ISLANDS

FAST FACT

If you like the idea of floating islands in the sky, check out the amazing *Avatar* film series or the incredible Studio Ghibli fantasy film, *Howl's Moving Castle*.

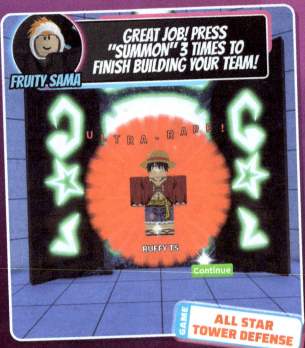

GAME — WORLD // ZERO

GET LOST IN A FANTASY ADVENTURE

46 Here, we explore a fantasy world, embarking on many adventures with a trusty pet at our side. Explore multiple realms and interact with other characters, who will offer you the chance to participate in quests. Collect items to help you on your way, and gather coins to level up.

GAME — ALL STAR TOWER DEFENSE

DEFEND YOUR TOWER

44 This is a great-looking game in which you have to protect your tower from attacking mobs and collect items as you progress. There are loads of characters to interact with and lots of places to explore, as well as defence codes that will help you level up. This is one of the most popular games on Roblox, with new features being added all the time.

GAME — ROYALE HIGH

HEAD TO SCHOOL

47 You can read all about the awesome Royale High game elsewhere here – this is just a taster! In this roleplaying game, the original idea was to play as a glittering fairy, and a lot of players do just that even though many other roles have been adopted. There are quests to complete, events to attend, and a leaderboard to keep track of how you're doing. You have your own phone with which you can send texts to friends in the game. You can collect diamonds to use for buying items, go shopping and teleport to different realms – and of course, you can fly! Getting to choose amazing outfits is a lot of fun, and the graphics are super-cute in a very Disney fairy-tale style.

GAME — ROBEATS

BECOME A ROCK STAR

45 This is a rhythm game that you'll need to play on your computer keyboard, as it just doesn't work as well on a mobile phone. In Robeats, you compete in rhythmic challenges that ultimately lead you to fame and fortune. You can play solo or with up to four friends, and there are tonnes of dance battles to try to beat as you become a Robeats rock star!

BECOME A SCIENCE WHIZ

48 In this game, you're a scientist who has to complete research in order to level up pets. This will enable you to upgrade your rank and compete on a leaderboard to become the best scientist around. Perform experiments and hatch your eggs into incredible creatures, collect gems so you can buy more pets, and upgrade in rank to move on to the next world.

GAME
SCIENCE SIMULATOR

Camila

COLLECT SQUISHMALLOWS

49 Here, we head to a Squishmallows store to stock up on these little cuties. It's just like the arcade game in real life, where you use a grabber to lift your pets out of their container – take care of them and they'll follow you around in their cute little way. Extra minigames add value here.

GAME
SQUISHMALLOWS

FAST FACT

Squishmallows are real-life plush toys that have been on the market since 2017. There are over 1,000 of these little friends to collect!

BECOME A FELINE!

50 This game is based on the concept of clans of feral cats living in the woods and enjoying a series of adventures. Want some of that? Heck yes, so here you can become part of that world, hunting and interacting with others. The woods where they live are beautiful, and you can create your cat avatar from scratch (get it?).

WARRIOR CATS: ULTIMATE EDITION

TOP 10 OBBYS

Prove your platforming skill in these classic Roblox obstacle course games

ESCAPE MEGA OBBY

1 Escape Mega Obby might be the peak of classic obby games. It's got it all – narrow beams to walk across, disappearing platforms, rainbow spiral stairs and some serious tests of skill – and it expertly moves from basic, easy obstacles through to tough ones that will make you work hard. If you only finish off one obby, this is the one to do.

THE DROPPER

2 Droppers are a different take on the obby, giving you tricky sections where you fall through a massive hole crammed with deadly obstacles and have to steer your way through. This one's massive, with over 120 themed levels, while the obstacles get stranger as the game goes on.

PARKOUR RUN

3 The great thing about Parkour Run is that it's so unpredictable. Every five minutes it puts together a course, and it's your job to make your way through before the clock runs down.

ESCAPE SCHOOL OBBY

4 Who doesn't like a great escape obby? No points for guessing what you're escaping from, but you might be surprised where you'll end up, with sections that'll take you through underground sewers, alternate dimensions and – worst of all – the gym! And don't let yourself get trapped by the teachers.

I'VE BLEACHED THE GYM FLOORS SO MAKE SURE NOT TO FALL!! >:)

ULTIMATE EASY OBBY

5 This one does exactly what it says it does, giving you an obby so easy that your grandad could do it, but with enough length to make you feel like you've achieved something.

TOWER OF HELL

6 This might be your perfect obby – if you like to spend your hours shouting at the screen. It's another obby where the course changes at random every five minutes, putting the pressure on to clear it fast. Some of the obstacles involve perfect jumping and perfect timing, and there aren't any checkpoints when you get it wrong.

COTTON OBBY

7 If you've been driven to tears by other obbys, this one should calm you right down. There are still some challenging sections, but it starts off easy and only slowly gets tricky, and the nice colour schemes and laid-back style make it a weirdly relaxing experience. It's also a brilliant obby for when you want to hang out with your friends.

AMAZING SPY MISSION

8 So, you fancy yourself as a James Bond or *Mission: Impossible*'s Ethan Hunt? This obby gives you the chance to prove it, with a series of vaguely spy-themed challenges and some sharp suits to try on. It's a little on the short and easy side, but it's a cracking obby while it lasts.

ESCAPE EVIL GRANDPA

9 No list of obbys would be complete without a game where you have to escape a murderous OAP. Like all the best examples, this one's weird, scary and sometimes disgusting, yet oddly lovable. Some sections might take you a while to work out, so pay attention to the scenery and keep exploring if you get stuck.

FAST FACT

Obbys have been around for almost as long as people have been playing Roblox. The first is reckoned to be Waffleboy's Obstacle Course all the way back in 2007!

EASY STUD JUMPS OBBY

10 This might look easy, but there's more to it than you think! All you need to do is get up a series of big steps, but as they get bigger, you won't be able to make the next on your own. Instead, you need to let the other players stand on you and jump, and trust they'll do the same!

3 WAYS TO BEAT OBBYS FASTER

Sick of getting stuck? Don't give up – get smart!

1 USE A CONTROLLER

Obbys are easier with a controller. The analogue stick is better than keys and mouse for walking narrow paths, and it's easy to change your point of view.

2 IT'S ALL ABOUT TIMING

Many obstacles involve avoiding moving blocks or beams. Learn how to time your moves to get as much time as possible to cross the danger zone or jump across a gap.

3 LEARN FROM THE EXPERTS

Stuck? Watch what the faster, more experienced players do. They'll know where to go and how to get past the more challenging obstacles. Give it time, and you'll become an expert too!

FAST FACT

Without a building gamepass, you can build on a one-storey, 30x30 plot, but a Multiple Floors pass allows you to build up to five floors high.

WELCOME TO BLOXBURG

Let's head to the big city!

Looking for a place where you can build your dream home, get a fun job and live a great life? Then dive into Welcome To Bloxburg, a simulation of life at home and work near a cool city. If you've ever played one of the *Sims* games, you know what you're in for, but for anyone new to this cool experience, read on for the ultimate guide to life in Bloxburg.

Sure, it will cost you 25 Robux to access the game, and even though it's been online for nearly a decade, it's still in beta, but we think you'll still have a great time building your house, interacting with other Bloxburgers and exploring the sights of the city. Over 5 billion people have

played Welcome To Bloxburg since it launched, and we can see why, with a ton of customisable building elements and up to 12 careers that you can pursue to build your store of Robux. Ready to go? Just follow us...

TOP 5 BLOXBURG JOBS

Earn cash in Bloxburg with these top jobs

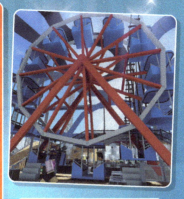

PIZZA PLANET

1 Serve pizzas and soda to customers with a smile at this cool restaurant, but remember – drinks cost $5 and pizza slices are $6 each. You can also deliver whole pizzas to players' houses for $35, and if you're lucky, Pizza Planet will offer you a job as a baker.

JANITOR FOR GREEN CLEAN

2 Use your broomstick to clean up rubbish from the ground and wash away the graffiti on buildings. Just like in real life, garbage replenishes itself quickly, so keep an eye out for those piles of rubbish and take care of them before Bloxburg starts to look messy.

BEN'S ICE CREAM

3 When a customer walks up to Ben's – an ice-cream cone-shaped building – and gives you their order, your job is to supply them with any of three flavours of ice cream: strawberry, chocolate and vanilla. They can also ask for sprinkles, chocolate sauce and cookie dough. Don't wait too long, or they'll walk off.

FISHING EXPERT

4 Head to the Fishing Hut and they'll automatically give you a fishing rod to cast into the sea. When the float starts to sink, that means a fish has grabbed the bait, so pull it out quickly. If you've caught a fish, you'll be in the money. Keep watching that float!

CASHIER AT BLOXY BURGERS

5 Take orders from NPCs and choose the food that the customer wants, but don't mess up their order, or they'll walk out. Try to get it right and you'll soon be Employee of the Week. Bon appetit!

QUICK TIPS

EXCELLENT EMPLOYEE

Want to earn more money and get promoted? Pick up an Excellent Employee pass for 300 Robux!

MAGIC MOODS

Did you know that you earn more money if your Mood scores are high? Stay cheerful and your bank balance will look healthier.

ITALIAN STYLE

What's the highest-paid job in Bloxburg? Pizza delivery, of course, but you'll often find yourself travelling across the map to get those delicious dinners to your customers.

ALSO CHECK OUT

VESTERLA

In this cool open-world game, you can choose to be a hunter, a warrior or a magician. Complete tasks, defeat foes, raid dungeons and take on enemy bosses.

THEME PARK TYCOON 2

In this city, you can only survive by earning money via completing quests. Once you've saved enough, you can build your own custom theme park!

THE PLAZA

Hang out with buddies in a cool apartment, play minigames, drive vehicles and explore this very cool map, which will be action-packed or relaxed, depending on your mood.

FOUR GREAT PLACES TO GO IN BLOXBURG!

Check out the best places to visit in Welcome To Bloxburg

BLOXBURG GYM

Looking to get athletic, boost your mood and build your muscles? Then head to Bloxburg Gym, a fully equipped fitness facility that you can find between the BFF Supermarket and City Hall. You don't have to pay to use the equipment, so head in and tackle those punchbags, free and machine weights and treadmills. You could even get fit in real life while playing Welcome To Bloxburg, if you have your computer set up in front of a fitness cycle!

FERRIS WHEEL

One of the coolest attractions in the whole of Bloxburg is its Ferris Wheel, located at the beach right next to the Fisherman's Hut – you could even take a ride on it to relax after a hard day of working on a fishing shift. The Ferris Wheel's function is to refill your and other players' moods, a job it does incredibly well. Of course, the view over the city is guaranteed to make anyone feel good. See you there.

STATS

OVER 5 BILLION PEOPLE have played Welcome To Bloxburg since 2014.

You have **FOUR KEY MOODS** to manage:

HUNGER, FUN, ENERGY & HYGIENE

On joining the game, you have a choice of

15 EMOTES TO DISPLAY

GAZBLOX

Welcome To Bloxburg is perfect for roleplay, and if you're considering a scenario in which you play a character who helps people get around the city, head to either of the two Gazblox gas stations. One of these can be found on the highway near the Campsite and also has a mini-mart, while the other is over in the town centre. Sure, cars don't need petrol to run, but this is where your roleplay skills come in useful, right?

COUNTRY LIVING

Looking to escape the city for a while? Then head to the Mountain, a barren area of wilderness that you climb via a twisty road. Once you're at the top, enjoy the view and the fresh air. If you want to stay outside Bloxburg for a while longer, check out the Campsite, which is complete with tents and a fire. You can stay there until your house is ready for you to live in, as there's no charge. Find it on the road above Riverside, near Gazblox.

FAST FACT

When you begin building your property, a black transparent wall surrounds your plot, which other players can't enter. Super useful!

WHY I LOVE... WELCOME TO BLOXBURG

GRACE

Welcome To Bloxburg lets you carry out tasks such as working, building your dream home, exploring and role-playing with friends! My favourite activities involve creating new home designs and inventive role-plays, as well as taking my kids for a walk to the top of the Bloxburgian cliffs. I also like the festival updates with food stands and firework booths and new emotes.

TOP 10 SIMS

Ten of the best simulation experiences on Roblox

PET SIMULATOR X

1 In real life, you don't usually have that many pets available – we reckon most people go for a dog, a cat or a rabbit, or maybe something slightly exotic like an iguana. In Pet Simulator X, though, you have up to 180 animals to choose from. Create a family of critters, keep them well fed and give them lots of affection, and don't forget walkies!

Golden Bunny
Basic

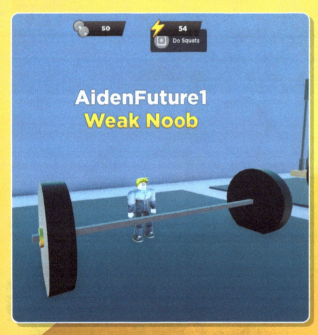

GLIDER SIMULATOR

2 Let's get off the ground and fly for a change – after all, the Roblox landscape is a beautiful sight from the air, especially once you're up in a noise-free glider. Mind you, we don't just wander around the clouds in this sim; our goal is to collect coins, gems and other goodies, and use them to upgrade our aircraft. We're literally getting our wings.

AidenFuture1
Weak Noob

YOU CAN BUY A NEW PICKAXE!

STRONGMAN SIMULATOR

3 Feeling athletic today? Build up those muscles with this excellent power-lifting sim, working on your strength every day by performing multiple lifts of a number of weights, from the manageable to the massive. To progress through the game, you'll have to be strong enough to move obstacles out of your way – a leaderboard provides the element of competition.

MINING CLICKER SIMULATOR

4 Get your pickaxe ready – we're going underground. Our job in Mining Clicker Simulator is to mine a bunch of different mineral ores that drop cash when you grab them. Once you're cashed up, you can use your newfound wealth to buy pets. Acquire enough of these friendly beasties, and you'll soon have an army of them to help you with the digging work.

WEAPON FIGHTING SIMULATOR

5 Build an arsenal of swords, armour, shields and other useful weaponry, and you'll be the toughest competitor in this fun sim. Add a range of magic spells to your arsenal and you'll be unstoppable as you wander the many Realms of this sim, defeating a range of adversaries.

TOWER DEFENSE SIMULATOR

6 Build your tower and enjoy the view. Wait – who's that on the horizon? It looks like a wave of zombies, so fortify your defences, build up an army, and have that sword ready. You can invite friends to join you in multiplayer mode and work together to build up your tower's strength.

CLICKER SIMULATOR

7 Get your clicking finger warmed up before you play this sim, because it's going to get a workout. Travel the map and click to earn rewards, including a range of pets: these can be the usual domesticated animals or mythical creatures of legend. As you move through the game, new Realms are unlocked and upgrades appear.

MERGE SIMULATOR

9 Grab blocks and merge them in this simple sim, which might not sound that much fun, but it's strangely enjoyable! The more blocks you merge, the more currency they drop, and as you amass wealth you can use it to buy minions, who will help you with the block-merging. Pretty soon, you'll be the boss of a merging army.

SWORD FIGHTERS SIMULATOR

8 This sim allows you to collect a large arsenal of glittering swords, from the functional to the fabulous, and defeat a load of enemies and bosses. As you neutralise these threats, you'll find yourself showered with cash, which you can use to open pet eggs and unlock new weapons.

CHAMPION SIMULATOR

10 Not just another battle sim, Champion Simulator allows you to evolve your character with feats of strength and bravery, building up a store of gems. Sure, you'll be in combat against other Roblox warriors, so keep an eye out for their weaknesses and soon you'll be the victor. Look out for gems and upgrades.

TIPS FOR A GREAT SIM EXPERIENCE!

Want to get the most out of any Roblox sim game? Bear these key points in mind...

1 ANIMAL MAGIC
Pets are a big part of a lot of Roblox sims, and it's easy to build up a huge number of animals. Remember, they need your attention, and too many might contribute to game lag.

2 GRINDING GEARS
You may not be a fan of 'grinding' – repeating the same mindless in-game action to gain rewards. You might want to stick to sim games that offer an actual experience rather than just endless clicking.

3 DON'T SETTLE
Roblox has hundreds of sims, so don't spend too much time playing boring ones just for the sake of some gems. Move on to something more exciting, and the devs of the dull games will soon get the message that sims have to be fun!

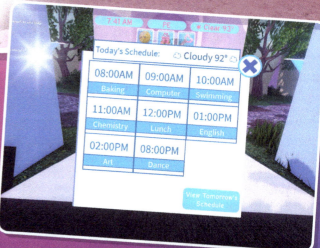

ROYALE HIGH

Where school is always cool

Visit Royale High for a school and roleplaying experience that allows you to play games, meet friends and take classes at school – without actually having to study! Thanks to the Universes feature on the Roblox platform, you can play in various Realms – in other words, a long list of cool and interesting environments where players can gather together to enjoy the fun. Grab your Teleportation Sceptre to travel at magical speed across the map and beyond!

Although the game was originally called Fairies & Mermaids Winx High School, the Royale High experience has expanded to include seasonal events. Make sure you and your friends put those dates in your diary, as they give you the chance to wear new costumes and meet buddies from around the world. If only school was this much fun in real life!

TOP 5 ROYALE HIGH REALMS

The best places Royale High has to offer, both past and present

AUTUMN TOWN

1 Between 2017 and 2020, Halloween wasn't Halloween unless you visited Autumn Town, a Realm containing houses where you could trick or treat the inhabitants. You could also bob for apples and buy autumn-themed items.

FANTASIA GETAWAY RESORT

2 Head to this luxury beach-side hotel and you'll never want to check out. As a side area game for the Royale High universe, this Realm lets players relax on a tropical island and meet others who just want a break from it all.

INTERGALACTIC TRADING HUB

3 Heading to outer space? Visit the Intergalactic Trading Hub via a UFO – found near the cinema – and also via the Teleportation Sceptre, passing through a cool cutscene on the way. It's only available to players over Level 75, though, so make sure you've worked your way up that far, or you won't get access.

SNOWGLOBE SUMMIT

4 Formerly known as Christmas Town, this was a Christmas-themed Realm from 2019 to 2022 – so will it come back this year? We hope so, because it offers us cool diamonds shaped like snowflakes and stashed in multiple chests.

WICKERY CLIFFS

5 This cool but sadly temporary Realm was live from October to November 2021. We're hoping it comes back, because its autumnal cliffside town was one of the most attractive Realms ever to appear in Royale High. If not, never fear – there are dozens more live Realms to enjoy!

QUICK TIPS

HIGH LIFE
If you want to make money in Royale High, participate in events – these give you the chance to earn diamonds and other cool rewards.

OFFLOAD YOUR ITEMS
Sell stuff you don't need – you can earn money by selling items you no longer want, especially if their value has increased since you bought them.

GAME ON
Royale High contains several minigames that allow winners to earn money and diamonds. Keep an eye out for these opportunities and you'll soon increase your Robux balance!

ALSO CHECK OUT

WEDNESDAY ADDAMS STORY
Head to Nevermore Academy for the mysterious events taking place within. Help Wednesday defeat the monsters and save the day!

ROBLOX HIGH SCHOOL
You and between four and 12 students are studying hard at school together, but this open-world multiplayer lets up to 50 more log onto a single server.

AKADEMI HIGH SCHOOL
This spooky game follows Ayano Aishi, also known as Yandere-chan, a schoolgirl who falls in love with another student. Don't get in her way.

TIME FOR SCHOOL

GET SOME FRESH AIR

Sure, Royale High is all about doing well at school and having fun at the same time, but it's not all about books and homework. One of the things we like most about this experience is the beautiful outdoor environment, like the trees and park we see here.

Computer class is starting!

STAY ON TIME

Keep an eye out for this green banner – it will pop out of your screen and remind you when classes are about to start, as well as other useful reminders. The only problem is you may be having too much fun with everything else on the map to find time for school!

HEAD TO CLASS

Why don't all schools look as fun as this? When it's time for class, head to your locker and get the right book for each subject, otherwise it's going to be difficult to pass the course. Remember, high grades mean lots of diamonds and other goodies! Better start studying...

DRESS FOR SUCCESS

Remember, you don't have to stick with the default skin we've chosen for our little avatar friend. In Royale High, there are no limits to what you can wear, and your choices aren't limited to fairy and princess costumes either. Be imaginative – the sky is the limit here!

MAKE A CALL

If you need to emote or change your clothes, the Royale High mobile phone is a lot better than the real-world equivalent – it can do it all for you. Just click on the phone, and it will expand to fill the middle of your screen, where it will be ready to do your bidding.

Cell Phone

50

Dress Up!

Emotes

Shopping

Teleport

WHY I LOVE... ROYALE HIGH

CHLOE

This dreamy and majestic game has so many things to do in it, it's so fun! You get to dress-up and I love showing off my personality with the things I wear! You can also explore the world and my all-time favourite place to go to is the Royale High School, where you can make new friends, focus on your studies and earn diamonds, which you can use to buy new accessories.

TOP 10

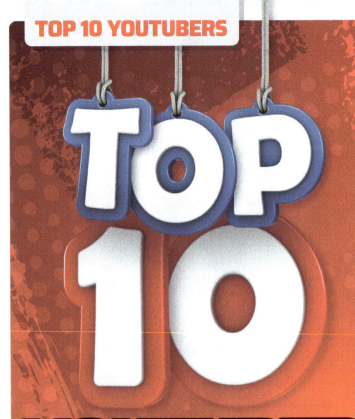

YOUTUBERS

Meet the online stars of Roblox royalty!

KAWAII KUNICORN
@KAWAIIKUNICORN

2 How could you not click on a video called 'Donut Heist – how I got my hands on the perfect treat'? Kawaii Kunicorn shows us how to have fun with friends and food in this celebratory collection devoted to living your best life in Roblox. There's slightly mad stuff too, like 'Survival Against The Evil Doctor's Zombie Curse!'

LANKYBOX @LANKYBOX

3 This channel has over 24 million subscribers and 7,000 videos, thanks to the fact that it's made by a collective of filmmakers rather than a single creator. Foxy, Boxy, Ghosty, Rocky, the excellently named Thicc Shark and others focus on quirky rather than instructional clips: we particularly liked 'We spent $1,000,000 Robux!' from April 2023.

LILLEPEKKA @LILLEPEKKA

1 This YouTuber's midsized channel – 50 videos, a million or so subs – mainly focuses on 'Best Moments' and 'Funniest Moments' compilations from their Roblox experiences. This makes the channel easy viewing – the perfect way to unwind after a long day in the real world. Channels like this one remind you how funny Roblox can be.

PEACHYYLEXI
@PEACHYYLEXI

4 In this channel devoted to the lives and times of a Roblox family, Peachyy Lexi shows us what her parents and kids get up to, takes us shopping and on visits to friends, and even shows us what happens when she decides to run for Mayor of Bloxburg. Along the way, we bump into a cast of colourful characters.

SKETCH @SKETCH

5 Here's the weird side of Roblox, with videos of chair-throwing, burning cars, flying planes and more – all of which remind us that crazy stuff can and will happen on our favourite game platform. The 'Roblox Psychic Playground' video is a suitably nutty starting point: where does this YouTuber get all these surreal ideas from?

POP DOG ROBLOX
@POPDOGROBLOX

6 Looking for speedruns? This YouTuber has made a bunch of attempts to complete various games and achievements in record time. We expect he's equipped with a state-of-the-art computer and high-speed internet, because any game lag would seriously ruin his channel.

FLAMINGO
@FLAMINGO

7 'This Roblox trend is disturbing' and 'Banned from Roblox retirement home' are two of Flamingo's videos, which make him sound like he's not a fan. However, with 15 years of Robloxing behind him, we think he's just a die-hard fan who wants Roblox to be perfect.

FAST FACT

The official @Roblox YouTube channel was launched in 2006 and now has 4 million subscribers and over 182 million views.

MACKENZIE TURNER ROBLOX
@MACKENZIETURNERROBLOX

8 'I went vegan for a month in Roblox!' is just one of Mackenzie Turner's videos that made us chuckle. This YouTuber seeks out the funny side of Roblox, showing us how to make the most of its multiplayer games.

NOBZI
@NOBZI-OL1ZQ

9 Scary prison officers, spooky demons and evil grandmas all populate Nobzi's videos, so be prepared for the occasional jump-scare. Still, he reminds us that Roblox is also the perfect platform for action-adventure games.

LANA'S LIFE
@LANASLIFEEE

10 Lana doesn't just explore Roblox; she takes us to real-world events, such as a game developers' conference, and cooks up a batch of Roblox-themed cakes. She interacts with other players, takes part in roleplays and makes sure we get a peek into this world.

BECOME A ROBLOX YOUTUBER!

Want to be a Roblox content creator? Here's how to get started!

1 BE INTERESTING!
In a world with millions of YouTube channels, make yours stand out. Have something to say, explain your viewpoint persuasively and use visuals creatively.

2 THUMBS UP
Make sure your video thumbnails are eye-catching – you want to attract fellow Roblox fans. There are online courses that show how to do this, or just ask a computer-savvy friend or family member.

3 SAFETY FIRST!
There's a lot of adult language on YouTube, as well as laws that govern who can and can't use and create channels, so get parental permission where necessary and don't engage with trolls. Remember to get some fresh air, too!

FAST FACT

The game had an extra map – Cursed Cavern – during the limited time Buried Treasure event. If you found the hidden ring you could win an eye-patch!

HIDE AND SEEK EXTREME

Everyone's favourite Hide and Seek

Sure, you've played Hide and Seek, but have you ever played it like this? Forget trying to sneak behind the sofa or lurk behind a wall in the playground while your mate counts from one to ten. Here, you've got 60 seconds to find a top hiding spot, and you're a mouse-sized player doing their best to stay unnoticed in spaces in and around the average house. Can you stay undiscovered in the kitchen, or avoid detection in the bedroom or the attic? Can you escape the seeker in the garden, or are you going to get caught?

Of course, for Hide and Seek to work, somebody has to play 'It'. You're frozen on the spot for the first minute, but after that you need to hunt down the other players. Luckily, each 'It'

character has a special skill you can use to find the hiders. You can sprint after anyone you catch running away, or spread a spot of glue to hold them in place so you can grab them!

TOP **5** HIDING SPOTS

Live to fight another day with these essential hiding places

INSIDE THE OVEN

1 When you're in the kitchen, the open oven is an obvious place to hide. Beneath the lower oven shelf, there's a secret compartment where you can't be spotted. Clued-in seekers might get you, but noobs won't have a hope!

ON TOP OF THE WHITEBOARD

2 A sneaky teleport pad on the blue beam near the spawn point in the Workshop will take you straight to the top of the whiteboard. Extra-cheeky players can even drop down to the board eraser.

UP THE TREE

3 It's just about possible to climb up the trees in the Garden, but smart players will know about the teleport pad under the plant in the corner by the tallest tree. Jump on it and you'll get dropped right at the top!

BEHIND THE PAINTING

4 The higher you go in the Attic, the better the hiding spots get. Some players love to lurk on top of the weights or hide out in the pool table, but there's a great spot behind the painting, right in the rafters at the top.

UNDERNEATH THE PILLOW

5 The shelves have some places to hide in Ethan's Bedroom, but we can't resist the bed! Climb the white ladder, then head for the pillow. You'll drop through and teleport to a shelf – teleport back to hide beneath it.

QUICK TIPS

HIDE AND PEEK
Remember you can switch to the seeker's view while you're hiding. You can keep an eye on where they are – and work out when to make a run for another hiding spot.

STAY STILL
If you move, you're easier to spot and hear. Try to stay still as much as possible, and only run around when the seeker is distracted or you have no other choice!

FIND A HIGH SPOT
You're much easier to find and catch on the floor. Try to make it to a high spot where you can stay hidden and out of reach.

ALSO CHECK OUT

MEGA HIDE AND SEEK
Inspired by Hide and Seek Extreme, Mega Hide and Seek goes even crazier with cannons and slides to get you around and some ingenious maps.

PROP HUNT! HIDE AND SEEK
It's hunters vs ghosts in this cracking Prop Hunt game, where the ghosts can transform into everyday objects to stay hidden from the hunters.

PROP HUNT X HIDE VS SEEK
Turn into an object in order to stay hidden. Get caught and you turn into a seeker. Can you keep hiding until the end?

Don't let them get away!

TOP 10 TIPS
FOR SEEKERS

USE YOUR SKILLS

2 Every It character has an ability, which you can activate by pressing the A button or mouse key. Glue can stop a getaway, while spring is great for catching players. Don't let them escape!

LISTEN UP

3 You should look for players and any signs of movement, but don't forget to use your ears as well! Hiders can't help making footsteps when they move, and with headphones on you can sometimes hear where they're hiding when they taunt you.

LOOK AROUND YOU

1 Remember, you can move the camera while you're hunting down those hiders. Look around to see if anyone is running around behind you, and keep an eye out for any sudden moves.

FAST FACT

The Yeti 'It' character has a unique Stun ability. It has a club that sends out shockwaves that stuns any hider it touches.

STATS

OVER
11,000
active players

OVER **6** MILLION
Favorites

OVER
**2.2 BILLION
VISITS**

CHECK THE TOP SPOTS

4 Do you know most of the top hiding spots? You can bet that the other players will as well. Check them out as you make your way around the map. If you're lucky, you can find two players at once!

GET TO KNOW THE MAPS

5 The more you play Hide and Seek Extreme, the better you'll know the map. Find the jump pads and teleport pads and where they can take you. It'll be easier to find hiding players.

PLAY SMART

6 Blunder around the map from one end to the other, and you'll use up your time without finding anyone. Think about the best way to cover all of the different areas and use short cuts and jumps to get around a little faster.

CATCH THEM QUICKLY

7 When you spot them, hiding players will usually make a run for it. Chase them, but try to avoid running around in circles around obstacles or objects. If they try it, stop, turn around and surprise them!

WATCH AND LEARN

8 Some players are good at playing 'It', so when you're found, watch them. Do they have any tricks for spotting players, or have they found hiding spots? Watch and you might learn something!

GET A BETTER VIEW

9 It's hard to see what's happening from ground level, so use the jump and teleport pads. You can look around and see players hiding behind big objects. That's your chance to track them down.

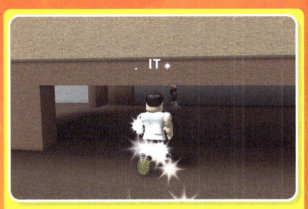

DON'T GIVE UP

10 Sometimes playing 'It' is tough, so don't get sad if you don't find anyone in the first minute. Take your time and follow the tips above, and you're bound to catch a couple of players. The more you seek, the better you'll get.

WHY I LOVE... HIDE AND SEEK EXTREME

JAMES

I really like Hide And Seek Extreme because there are lots of different maps. My favourite map is the garden, but my favourite hiding space is the vending machine. I love being the hider and trying to find cool new hiding spots.

TOP 10 SHOOTERS

Looking for action?
Get these games in your sights

PHANTOM FORCES

1 For years, Phantom Forces has been Roblox's answer to classic *Call Of Duty*, dishing out awesome action match after match. Seeing two teams, the Phantoms and the Ghosts, duke it out across a range of mighty maps, it has the kind of customisable weapons and advanced moves that you'd expect to see from a big console FPS.

ZOMBIE OUTBREAK

2 Fighting the living is hard enough, but how about the dead? Inspired by *Call Of Duty*'s Zombie mode, Zombie Outbreak pits you and your team against waves of hungry zombies and their scary monster bosses. Upgrade your guns and keep an eye on your ammo; you're going to need every bullet you can get!

BAD BUSINESS

3 Looking for a shooter you can really get your teeth into? Bad Business is as cool and competitive as they come. It's got dozens of guns to gear up with and a brilliant prestige system, where you can unlock new tiers of weapons to add to your load-out. Make sure you're ready for a challenge.

ARSENAL

4 Is this the ultimate gun game? You start with a random weapon, and with each kill it's switched for a different one. Your mission is to make it through the list and grab a kill with the final gun. Going from assault rifle to catapult, you never know what's coming, but it's going to be fun!

FRONTLINES

5 Frontlines is an all-action shooter with some serious eye candy. It looks like a modern FPS, and plays like one, with team-based game modes and weapons straight from *Call Of Duty* or *Battlefield*. Just be warned – it's tough!

BIG PAINTBALL

6 You can swap bullets and body counts for paint splats and fun in this colourful paintball shooter. This one goes big on great-looking maps and deadly gadgets, where you can trap your enemies with a paintball turret or find ways to surprise them. It still crams in a range of sniper rifles and paintball SMGs to mix things up.

TRENCHES

7 Two teams of 25 struggle for victory, building fortifications, wrecking the other side's defences and blasting at their forces before they can overrun yours. It's a frantic shooter on the surface, but this has surprising depths.

FAST FACT

The biggest Roblox FPS games can build up a massive fanbase. Over 10 million players have favoured Arsenal, and it's had over 4.6 billion visits!

SHOOT OUT

8 Most shooters take a theme and stick with it, but Shoot Out tries to pack them all in! This is the game where you could be gunning down varmints as a cowboy in a western saloon in one round, then battling it out as killer robots in the next. Best of all, it keeps changing, with new heroes, villains, maps and weapons appearing all the time.

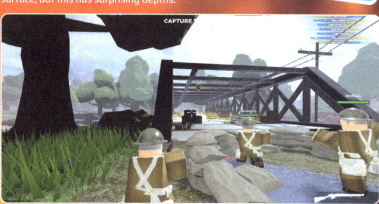

ENERGY ASSAULT

9 It's all about energy weapons in this fast-paced FPS, but the maps head off the sci-fi track with modes and maps inspired by *Call Of Duty* and *Counter-Strike*, plus strolls into the countryside or the canals of Venice. It's worth playing just for the Hill Control and Domination modes, where holding the control points is more important than getting kills.

AIMBLOX

10 Aimblox is one of the most exciting Roblox shooters of the last few years, combining classic competitive action with a brilliant co-op mode, where you can train your aim by tackling evil drones and rescuing captured civilians. You've got a superb selection of guns to blast away with, and it's a great shooter for noobs looking to build up their skills.

3 WAYS TO FIX YOUR KILL/DEATH RATIO

It's kill or get killed, and you're dying every time. It's time to sort it out!

1  **AIM FOR THE CHEST**
Headshots are great for experts, but when you start, aim for the body. You'll have more chance of hitting your target and not getting killed.

2  **DO YOUR HOMEWORK**
Focus on one game and get to know the controls, weapons and maps. You'll work out the routes players follow, the best spots to shoot from and ways to sneak up on them.

3 **BECOME A HARD TARGET**
Don't just stand there and shoot! Learn how to strafe, moving from side to side while you keep the enemy in your sights. Crouching can also make you harder to hit, especially if there's cover!

WAITING FOR YOUR TURN

HEARTS4LOLAX

ENMAAAA

MURDER MYSTERY

Can you uncover the killer?

FAST FACT

The sheriff is the only one armed with a gun. The murderer's weapon of choice is a knife.

Murder Mystery 2 is one of those old-school Roblox games that seems to have been around forever. Compete as a murderer, sheriff or innocent, with the added twist that nobody knows who the murderer is. Together, the innocents must identify the murderer, while the murderer must try to kill everyone else. The sheriff's job is to find the killer and eliminate them.

The game features a wide range of tools that players can use to defend themselves, but perks or powers are what really help you rise to the top. Skins change the appearance of a player's character and can be sold for large amounts of in-game currency, which is earned by completing various tasks and missions.

This player-led game has really gained popularity due to its social interactions. Can you solve the mystery and survive each round?

TOP 5 MAPS RANKED

The best locations to run around in

FACTORY

1 Factory is one of the largest maps in the game. There are various hiding spots, which makes life harder for the murderer. Players can also climb into tubes that frame the doorway. Some hiding spots are widely known among the gaming community, but others have remained under wraps.

POLICE STATION

2 Police Station is a large map with different rooms, hallways and vents that all make for good places to hide from the murderer. Innocents can also stow away in the toilets, on top of the shooting range bars, or inside a yellow car that's parked in the garage.

BIO LAB

3 Another one of the biggest maps is the Bio Lab, which comprises vents, an office, a room containing bio-tubes, a workshop, two storage rooms and a centre area with a vast grey tube. Inside the secret area, there is a dummy that you can hide behind.

WORKPLACE

4 Workplace is one of the oldest maps in the game, which is why it doesn't have that many places to hide. You have a choice of office space, kitchens, hallways and plenty of dead ends, which often causes widespread panic among the innocents if a chase is afoot.

MANSION 2

5 Mansion 2 is a remake of the old mansion map (with added hiding spots for the innocents) and is built in such a way that it's suitable for all three roles. Some good hiding spots are inside the fridge and behind the closet next to the garage.

QUICK TIPS

FIND THE SHERIFF

As the sheriff is the only player that has a gun, it is in your best interests to make sure they are always nearby. Just watch out if they're shooting.

BE CAREFUL WHO YOU TRUST

As the murderer, tricking others into believing that you are an innocent is a great tactic. As the sheriff, it's also an incentive to force the murderer to take action.

FORM ALLIANCES

Talk to other players and form alliances. This can help you to gather resources and information, increasing your chances of solving the mystery.

ALSO CHECK OUT

IDENTITY FRAUD

If you enjoy maze games, this is the one to try. There are only a few stages, and in each one there's a large and terrifying monster waiting around every corner.

ALONE IN A DARK HOUSE

Play as a private investigator, assigned with testing your detective smarts by solving a vehicle murder in a small town. The plot thickens later on.

IMPOSTOR

Can you find the imposter? Expect to witness some unexpected reveals and moments that will have you holding your breath for the worst that could happen.

THE FOUR COOLEST

NIGHTFIRE

Nightfire is classified as a rare gun in Murder Mystery. The gun's barrel has a bright pink colour that blends into a navy blue barrel, giving it a pretty unique look compared to other guns. It has a companion knife named Space as well, with which it shares several visual characteristics. Nightfire can be acquired by unwrapping a Mystery Box, and can be traded for an estimated value of 1-4 Tier 1 firearms or knives.

3m 0s

STATS

First released in 2014, the game has close to

10 BILLION VISITS AND 5 MILLION LIKES

IT CONSISTS OF
12 **players**
1 **murderer**
1 **sheriff and**
10 **innocents**

If you're looking for the highest valued item, **Nik's Scythe** goes up to

150,000
Seers or more.

LASER

Laser is a Godly gun that's ideal for anyone who loves weapons that look like they were made in the future. It's based on a real-life laser-tag gun and is shown with a red and black colour scheme - the trigger and grip are black, and the rest of the gun is red. To get this weapon, players must first unlock Gun Box 3. Despite an estimated market worth of 55 Seers, some players will sell this rifle for more than 60.

Survival XP
80

FAST FACT

If you have a radio, the murderer can track where you are by the sound, increasing your chances of getting murdered.

GUNS

Get your hands on these great guns for the best chance of taking out the murderer

CHROMA LIGHTBRINGER

The Chroma Lightbringer is probably the best-looking gun in the game. It's part of the Chroma Bringer Set, which also includes the counterpart gun, Chroma Darkbringer. It can be obtained by opening Mystery Box 2. The entire model is white with Chroma-effect patches. The trigger, wing, barrel and a tiny patch on the handle are all Chroma. A wing on top of its grip gives it a cool appearance when held.

ELDERWOOD REVOLVER

The Elderwood Revolver was first available in the special Halloween Box during the 2019 Halloween event. This firearm was introduced alongside the Elderwood Knife, completing the Elderwood set. A dark purple tree trunk was used to make the handle, and purple engravings adorn the barrel and frame. The Elderwood Revolver is estimated to be worth between 110 and 145 Seers. It's the ideal item for those who enjoy carrying a vintage revolver.

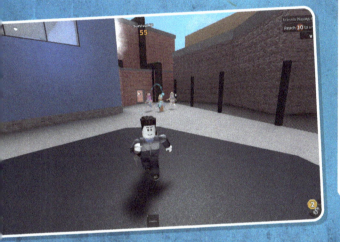

WHY I LOVE... MURDER MYSTERY

MAYA

Murder Mystery is one of my favourite games. I love being the murderer or sheriff, because it's even more fun if you have an important role! I also like the trading system because I love collecting Godly weapons and trading for even better valued ones! I would definitely recommend this game when you're looking for something fun to play with your friends.

Images: Wiki: Sottrasworld: Tres2345

59

TOP 10 ROLE-PLAYING GAMES

Get into character with these epic roles!

SUPER HERO LIFE III

2 Ever fancied being a superhero? Well, now you can be one – just design a costume and customise your superpowers, and you're ready for action. You can battle other characters in player-versus-player mode, although you risk dying if you come up against someone tougher or faster than you. Stick to RP mode for a safer campaign and a more relaxed experience!

ROCITIZENS

3 You're living in a large city, working a job, raising a family and buying goods from your local supermarket. In case this all sounds a little too much like real life, RoCitizens allows you to switch to criminal mode and rob banks – although, just like in real life, the police will catch you and stick you in prison!

HEROES ONLINE

1 It's Heroes versus Villains in this open-world map series. Which one will you choose: the noble life of a Hero, defending your fellow citizens and keeping public life safe and secure; or the fun but morally unsound existence of a Villain, stealing people's possessions and generally doing anything you can to avoid getting a job? Both sound appealing to us.

THE WILD WEST

4 As the title suggests, this allows you to play the part of a cowboy, outlaw or bounty hunter in the American West. Robbing banks and mining for gold are all part of a typical day in this huge, detailed map. Will you settle down on your own ranch, or make a buck by robbing passers-by? The choice is yours.

TERRARIA RPG

5 Everyone remembers the old 2D action game *Terraria*, released at the dawn of time (2011). Now, you can play it again as a Roblox RPG, with loads of added features. The goal of saving the planet remains the same, but you're given more enemies and more weapons to defeat them with. The original game's sense of humour is still intact, though.

ANOMIC

6 Uh-oh – a nuclear war has occurred, leaving you in a multiplayer role-playing game that requires you to survive in post-holocaust conditions. Law has been replaced by anarchy, so your best bet may be to become an outlaw. If you don't fancy the criminal lifestyle, get a job and work your way up the new social hierarchy. You'll need to keep your wits about you.

JAILBREAK

7 Evening, officer! In Jailbreak, you might want to play the role of a cop, preventing evildoers from being an all-round pain to everyone else in the game, or you might prefer to be a criminal, pulling off audacious heists and living it up like there's no tomorrow. In either role, you'll be in for a lot of car chases and plenty of high-octane excitement.

053 MPH **GUZZLER** 2 mi

DUNGEON QUEST

9 Feeling knightly today? Then get your armour on and strap on that sword – there are dungeons to explore and monsters to defeat! Dungeon Quest offers you the chance to inhabit the role of a Sir or Lady of your choice, collecting treasure, upgrading your weapons and taking on noble challenges. Invite your friends along and create a full Round Table.

FANTASTIC FRONTIER

8 This medieval open-world map equips you with a basic set of weapons and tools, but never fear; the more battles you win, the tougher you become. Along the way, NPCs will give you tasks to complete, each of which will reward you for your success. You'll meet some mythical creatures, too, so watch out!

BOKU NO ROBLOX

10 Ah, it's the eternal question of good versus evil – or rather, the question of 'Shall I destroy this planet with my evil powers, or shall I be the good guy for a change and prevent that from happening?' Either way, your character is powered by special assets called quirks. These will assist you along the way.

HOW TO EXCEL AT ROBLOX RPGS!

Follow these three golden rules to make the most of your role-playing

1 CHOOSE YOUR WEAPONS

Make a choice based on the map, its terrain and your enemies. Use magic, but sparingly – you never know when a spell or power-up will appear.

2 MAKE FRIENDS

Multiplayer RPGs may be your best bet if you're new to role-playing, as your more experienced friends can show you the ropes. Repay their help by helping them complete their campaigns.

3 LIVE TO FIGHT ANOTHER DAY

Don't be downhearted if a particular RPG isn't for you. Roblox has more roles to play than any of us could fit into a single lifetime, so if Role A isn't much fun, quit and play Role B or Role C instead!

FAST FACT

Structure your theme park with half gentle and half intense rides to attract a higher number of visitors.

THEME PARK TYCOON

Build the world's coolest theme park

It has been almost a decade since the highly acclaimed Theme Park Tycoon experience was launched on Roblox. It quickly became the platform's most popular tycoon-type game, probably because it was a lot of fun for users to experience and made loads of money for the biggest and best maps. With rollercoasters, ghost trains, fairground rides and more, the best parks were unforgettable.

Nowadays, there's an even more successful Theme Park Tycoon 2 experience for those who can't get enough of the life of a fairground owner: it's similar to the original game, so the advice below works for both versions. The key tip is the same in both cases: build a park that is fun to visit and people will be queuing up to get in. If you get it right, your park will become a money-maker, with a nice stream of Robux coming in. The word 'tycoon' is in the title for a reason!

TOP 5 THEME PARK RIDES

Our pick of the best rides for Roblox thrill-seekers!

ROLLERCOASTERS

1 What's a theme park without rollercoasters? Give your visitors the adrenaline rush of a lifetime with a variety of coaster types, made up of one, three, five or seven cars for legacy models and up to seven in the newer, improved-physics variants. Make sure you include banking at the corners!

GENTLE RIDES

2 Take it easy on younger or more timid visitors to your park with slower-moving rides, such as the classic revolving teacups that we all rode in as kids. You'll also find helter-skelters – or spiral slides for your American guests – as well as an observation tower, a roundabout (also known as a carousel) and even a gently rotating Ferris wheel.

INTENSE RIDES

3 Higher intensity comes with a higher nausea rating, unfortunately, so build your space rings, drop tower, swinging ship, fireball loop and slingshot ride – the last of these a physically impossible device, we hope – with a bit of caution. You don't want your visitors complaining about feeling seasick, after all.

WATER RIDES

4 Soak your visitors – or at least, leave them a bit damp – with a load of swan boats, a log flume, a river rapids experience and even a 'nautic jet' – they'll love it! The sound of shrieks and splashes is part and parcel of any visit to a theme park, and what's more, people will actually pay to get doused in water!

TRANSPORT RIDES

5 Not rides as such, but certainly items that your visitors can ride on, this category refers to the monorail and transport train that people use to get around the theme park. A hot tip is to allow people to walk around the park if they want, otherwise, the transport rides may get busy at peak times.

QUICK TIPS

SCENERY STYLE

You have a choice of hundreds of scenery pieces with which to decorate your park, so make sure you choose a wide selection to attract the eye. A pretty park is a popular park, right?

DESIGN WITH CARE

When you design your theme park, it's essential to include a path, lights, tables, seats, benches and bins, as well as a clear entrance and exit. People like ease and convenience!

MONEY MATTERS

If you want to be a Robux millionaire, you'll need to understand the psychology of your customers. For example, if you make your rollercoaster rides fairly short, did you know that people will pay to ride on them a second or third time? Give them what they want, but not all in one go.

ALSO CHECK OUT

ROBLOX POINT THEME PARK

With a dozen attractions and a selection of minigames – hey, is that table hockey? – the Robloxia park is one of the platform's most popular destinations. You can drive around it if you're feeling too tired to walk, too.

THRILLVILLE PARK

This theme park lives up to its name, with various rollercoasters, an obstacle course, a train ride and a face-changer. You can see it in action in the acclaimed Roblox Gone Crazy video series.

THEME PARK HEIDELAND

Inspired by a real-life theme park, this does a great job of emulating that attraction's thrills. Ride the rollercoasters, enjoy ice cream and check out the log flume!

FOUR COOL WAYS TO MAX OUT YOUR THEME PARK!

Make it a memorable experience with these top tips!

PAYING GUESTS

For extra income, add stalls to your park where visitors can buy food and drink, but don't make the goods too expensive, or they'll complain about the cost and never come back. Instead, aim for a few Robux per item, and your customers will feel that you care about their experience at your park. You can even install a restroom for their convenience – who doesn't appreciate a comfort break every now and then? The customer is always right, remember.

FAST FACT

A nausea rating might seem like a weird thing to enjoy, but some players find lots of queasy loops enjoyable!

THE NUMBERS GAME

If you're interested in finding out if your guests are really enjoying themselves at your theme park, you can do better than just hanging out by the entrance and seeing who's coming and going. For a more professional overview of your guests' experience, check their statistics. Your rating will reveal a lot, as will a detailed check of their feedback. Take their suggestions seriously, make improvements to your park as they come up, and watch your business profit.

SIX OF THE BEST

Did you know that Theme Park Tycoon 2 allows for up to six players and their respective theme parks, meaning that neighbouring players can visit the parks of other players in the same server? In other words, you're not just making money while you're at your park – you can nip next door for a fun-filled ride or two, just for a laugh. Furthermore, park owners can grant other players access to building rights, so a few of you can work on the same park.

GAMING THE SYSTEM

Don't forget to include the option of game passes for your guests. These aren't required, of course: your visitors can still enjoy themselves without shelling out extra. In fact, you need to be clear about that or they may feel that you're ripping them off. Instead, emphasise that a game pass will enhance their theme park visit, with achievements to hit that will add value to their experience. You, too, can benefit from their enhanced experience: if players have a better time in your park, they'll come back again and again.

STATS

Theme Park Tycoon has enjoyed over

A BILLION PLAYS

TPT2 has earned itself a player rating of more than...

88%

The average visitor spends about

20 MINUTES

WHY I LOVE... THEME PARK TYCOON

FINN

It's cool because you can create your own theme park! I like that there are lots of cool rides and shops – my favourites are the log flume and the ice cream stall!

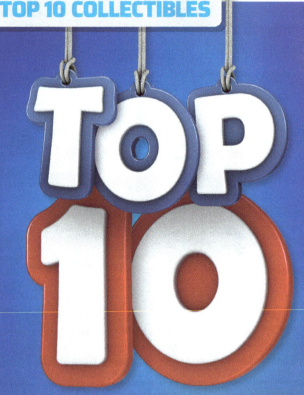

TOP 10

COLLECTIBLES

Collect these 10 valuable treasures and rule the Roblox world

DOMINO CROWN

1 Winners of the Domino Rally Building Contest back in the Stone Age (2007) nabbed a Domino Crown hat as a prize: there are either seven or 17 left in existence (depending on which source you believe) and they don't go on sale very often, for obvious reasons. We've seen prices of up to $187,500 for this lovely item of headwear.

ECCENTRIC SHOP TEACHER

2 The Eccentric Shop Teacher Hat was originally given to players as a prize in the Superheroes School Building Contest in 2010, and two years later one of its ten copies sold for about R$100,000. The prize was richly deserved, mind: to win one of these items you had to design a Roblox world filled with treasure, which players would rate. If you got a rating higher than 1,900, you bagged a Teacher Hat.

DOMINUS FRIGIDUS

3 The Dominus Frigidus hat holds the record for the largest purchase in Roblox history, selling in December 2022 to a user called mr_beanGuy for an astonishing 200 million Robux, the equivalent of around $700,000. Limited to only 26 copies, it was created by a user called Sethycakes whose wish from the Make-A-Wish Foundation was to visit Roblox HQ and design a hat.

CRIMSON THUG SHADES

4 There are only 14 copies left of the Crimson Thug Shades, so good luck tracking a pair down! Originally available as a 40-copy limited run, this tough item of eyewear originally cost R$625 – quite an outlay, you'll agree. Still, when the value rose to R$5,375 and then to a recent peak of R$38,652, anyone who splashed out at the original price would have congratulated themselves on a clever purchase.

GOLDLIKA: PATRIOT

5 Stick this around your avatar's neck and you'll attract lots of attention for sheer bling. Not everyone finds this item attractive, exactly, but heck, enough people want one for each of its 20 copies to sell for R$12,500. Only around half of those are still available, and if previous form is any indicator, their value will only increase.

THE KLEOS APHTHITON

6 Only ten of this mysterious item are said to exist, which makes it difficult to believe the average Roblox player when they boast of having seen one. There just aren't enough Kleos Aphthitons around for them all to be telling the truth! Still, if you see one on sale – you never know, right? – and you can afford to buy it (unlikely, we know), then snap it up, because it will certainly increase in value.

ANTENNA ANTLERS

7 Deer me! This cool accessory was offered as a prize to the winners of a Commercial Contest back in 2014, although there were only 15 at the time – and now there are far fewer. The last time an Antenna Antlers was seen on sale was in 2021, but don't expect to see one available again any time soon. The lowest listing we've seen allocated it a value of R$62,500, so save up.

LIVING ART: STARRY NIGHT

8 Stick your avatar's head through the middle of a classic masterpiece: that's what the Living Art: Starry Night artefact does if you pick one up for around $31,250. Mind you, that will be a rare occurrence: there were nine originally awarded to the winners of the 2013 Roblox Fan Art Contest, and the last time we saw one it was on sale for R$97,000.

THE WANWOOD CROWN

10 This Middle Ages-style headwear was originally awarded to the players who boasted the most visited locations in the Worlds of Wood Building Contest, and we have to admit, it looks pretty cool in a knightly sort of way. Where can we buy one, we hear you ask? Er, almost nowhere, unfortunately – and even if you find one, it'll cost you R$250,000.

BLACKVALK

9 What the heck? The Blackvalk has been seen on sale for almost five million Robux, even though it was launched in 2013 at around a tenth of that cost – 1,000,000 Tickets. Although you could briefly bag one at the price of 750,000 Tickets for the Roblox Presidents' Day Sale, few of us bothered, which was an error – because of the 264 copies sold, only 75 are still around now.

3 COLLECTIBLE CATEGORIES TO EXPLORE

Search within these brands for the individual artefact you've always dreamed of

1 FANCY FEDERATION

The ...Of The Federation range boasts three expensive hats, the Lord, Lady and Duke, valued at $125,000, $125,000 and $62,500 respectively.

2 DOMINUS DESIRABLES

Which Dominus hat will you go for? The Pittacium, for five million Tickets? The Empyreus, for 69 million Robux? Or the Astra, for 14 million Robux? Or you could just wear a bobble hat that cost a fiver, like us.

3 HEAVYWEIGHT HATS

In the Sparkle Fedora range, your eye will soon be caught by the Purple, Red and Orange variants. The Purple one costs around four million Robux; the Red counterpart is about the same; and the Orange version goes for nearly seven million Robux!

Café

MEEPCITY

The world is uniquely yours

With a variety of virtual worlds to get lost in, MeepCity is among the greats when it comes to Roblox experiences. Inspired by the now defunct Club Penguin, it boasts absolutely gigantic server sizes and countless things to do. Once you have exhausted your self-made virtual goals – decorated your first house, run a pizza place, taken care of your pet Meep – MeepCity's multiplayer servers allow you to venture forth to the community.

There are many tasks that reward you with coins when you want to earn some extra money. Fishing allows you to catch fish that you can sell in the Meep shop. Planting flowers in your home will give you plenty of coins, and you can also play minigames and complete quests as well. Dig deep enough, and you'll find everything you need to replicate whatever sits in your imagination on-screen. This is your chance to run a dance club or a pizza place, play minigames and complete quests, or adopt a pet Meep companion.

TOP 5 THINGS TO DO

The best ways to keep yourself amused in MeepCity

PLAY MINIGAMES

1 There are loads of minigames to enjoy in MeepCity, ranging from simple arcade games to more complex challenges and quests. Take a break from exploring and have some fun! It's also a chance to earn extra coins and rewards, so it's a win-win.

ADOPT A MEEP

2 You can buy a pet Meep for 100 coins. Just go to the pet shop at the playground, walk up to the counter and press 'Adopt a Meep'. Feed them, clean up after them and play with them to keep them happy. They'll surely return the favour!

GO FISHING

3 Fishing is a great way to relax, and you might even catch yourself a rare fish or two. You can fish at the docks, or you can go out on a boat and explore the open waters. This is a perfect activity to do with friends, so be sure to invite them along.

GO ON A DATE

4 Dating is a great way to get to know other players. You can go on dates by yourself, or you can invite friends to join you. Either way, it's a fun way to spend some time in MeepCity.

GET A JOB

5 One of the best ways to make some extra coins is to get a job. There are all sorts of jobs to choose from, so find one that interests you and get to work! Remember that you'll need the coins to buy things in the game, so it's a good idea to save up.

QUICK TIPS

GET TO KNOW THE MAP

MeepCity is a huge place, and it can be easy to get lost if you don't know your way around. Take some time to explore and learn the layout.

COINS ARE THE CURRENCY

You can find coins by completing quests, playing minigames, or just by exploring the city. One of the best ways to save up is to get a job.

CUSTOMISE YOUR MEEP

If you bought a Meep at the pet store, you can customise it to your liking by giving it a name, a colour and dressing it up.

ALSO CHECK OUT

ROYALE HIGH

Visit Royale High, make new friends and explore a school-based universe. The game has expanded to include seasonal events that players flock to every year.

WHISPERS OF THE ZONE

With a combination of interesting storylines and unique graphics, this presents a world of missions. Above all, it's one of the best open-world RPGs.

JAILBREAK

This sees players come out of prison and immediately embark on various missions, including obtaining a phone, robbing banks and stealing helicopters.

THE FOUR BEST ESTATES IN MEEPCITY

VICTORIAN ESTATE

Victorian Estate is one of MeepCity's biggest mansions and can be purchased through a blueprint from the Home Improvement Store in exchange for 999 Robux, which also makes it the game's most expensive. Aside from two floors and 14 spacious rooms, the house provides 17 pots outside the exterior of the house, which can be used for gardening. The estate is totally customisable, so use your imagination to create a beautiful residence.

STATS

MeepCity is one of the most popular Roblox games with over

15 BILLION VISITS

THE SERVERS SUPPORT UP TO

200 PLAYERS

(most Roblox games generally top out at around 30)

The Castle Estate is one of the most popular estates in the game. It can be acquired for

20,000
Meep Coins

CASTLE ESTATE

Castle Estate is also quite pricey, with a large number of rooms, but those interested must be willing to spend 20,000 Meep Coins to add it to their collection. Players can personalise the house and make use of the big space inside to live like a royal. The property looks like a small fortress from the outside due to its pointed domes and a large doorway.

WIZARD TOWER ESTATE

Wizard Tower Estate is the tallest estate in MeepCity. It's a four-storey property with nine rooms, all of which are large enough to give you plenty of options when it comes to making it your own. You might also want to tend to the 12 pots outside of the house. The Wizard Tower Estate is one of the most expensive in the game, costing 15,000 Meep Coins to purchase. After purchasing it, players can show it off to other online gamers.

HAPPY HOME PUMPKIN ESTATE

The Happy Home Pumpkin Estate was released during the 2019 Halloween special event. Players had to spend 7,500 Meep Coins or 3,750 Candies – the event currency – to purchase these pumpkin-themed digs. The Estate only has two storeys with two big rooms, making it ideal for hosting meetings. This estate can also be bought with 10,000 Meep Coins using a blueprint from the Home Improvement Store. Players with a pumpkin estate can make their own customisations to really make their estate stand out.

WHY I LOVE... MEEPCITY

ELIZA

MeepCity is really fun because there are lots of different places to visit. My favourite place is the school because there are different classes and you have to find the right one. I also like that you can get pet Meeps and change how you look!

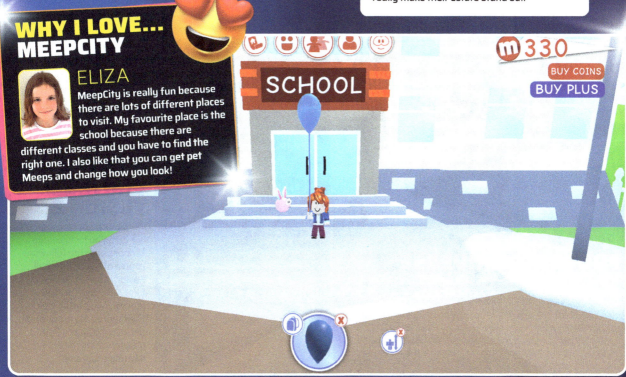

TOP 10

SPORTS

Win these essential sports games and take home all the prizes!

KICK OFF

2 Like the FIFA football games, Kick Off sees you control a team from a godlike position above the pitch. It's tricky to keep all the players on the right track, but that's the challenge that makes the game so compelling. Put the ball between the other's team's posts, and you'll be laughing all the way to the changing room.

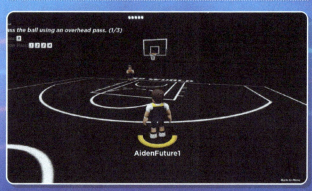

RB WORLD 4

3 Looking to shoot some hoops? Check out Anonymous Interactions' RB World 4, which entertains you with a bunch of cutscenes before loading up options. In this highly flexible map, you can play a short multiplayer game with friends, or take a moment to design your own player with a range of cool abilities.

HHCL LOBBY

4 If you're Canadian or know someone who is, you'll know how important ice hockey – or just hockey, as it's called in the Great White North – is to that nation. You'll love this hockey universe, which gives you options of major and minor league play, depending on how intense you want the game to be. Watch out for those goalside crunch attacks from burly players.

FOOTBALL FUSION 2

5 Launched in summer 2019, building a huge fanbase over the following couple of years, Football Fusion is one of Roblox's best American football games. Two captains pick their teams, flip a coin and decide who starts. Four quarters later, the winner will reign supreme.

FOOTBALL UNIVERSE

1 This massive game offers the American football fan everything they need to enjoy an online match, with items and players provided through a pack-based system. You can choose to play an NFL game with all the professional trimmings, or keep it simple and play at college level. Free codes will come your way the more you play, so keep an eye out!

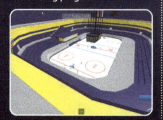

ROBLOX VOLLEYBALL 4.2

6 Volleyball is perfect for Roblox thanks to its landscape format and wide-angle play. One team launches the ball while the other responds, and players who spike the ball into their adversaries' half win. There's a Halt setting that slows the ball down for easier gameplay.

FAST FACT

Robloxers love sports. We know that because Wipeout Obby, a running/jumping course, has been played over 20 million times!

SUPER STRIKER LEAGUE

7 This one isn't just about scoring – it's about avoiding enemies that want to kill you! Avoid ninjas that shoot arrows, and stay out of the way of undead monsters. If you get past them, all you have to do is score.

ROBLOX DODGEBALL

8 You'll need to move fast to avoid getting squished by a fast-moving ball. In one mode, you're up against a team featuring a super-strong individual called the Juggernaut; in the other, you can be hit four times before you're out.

Welcome to Striker City!

Continue

PHENOM

9 If you've ever played the amazing basketball game NBA Phenom on the PlayStation 2 (remember that?), then you'll have a blast stalking the court and laying up a basket in Roblox's own version of this classic sports game. You can choose a team that's all ready to go, or take a moment to build your own custom squad, complete with players of your choice.

PSGA

10 The biggest gymnastics game on Roblox, the developers have worked tirelessly to represent the sport as accurately as possible. You have full access to a gymnasium, including vaults, uneven bars, balance beams, pommel horse and more. Practise routines or take part in classes and create the ultimate performance.

3 COOL TRICKS FOR SPORTS STARDOM

Watch the fine details and achieve more in Roblox sports

1 POWER ON
Keep an eye open for power-ups. These might appear on the ground or the air: use them to boost your ability numbers, which will enable you to increase your speed and energy.

2 STOP RIGHT THERE
If you're struggling with the speed of a game, check its play settings. In Normal mode, players and projectiles move at normal speed, but in Stop mode, you can make a ball slow down or stop completely.

3 IT'S A SETUP
When designing custom players, don't just make them as fast and strong as possible. Size, skill and even their cosmetic attributes may make them just as dangerous against an enemy team, depending on the game.

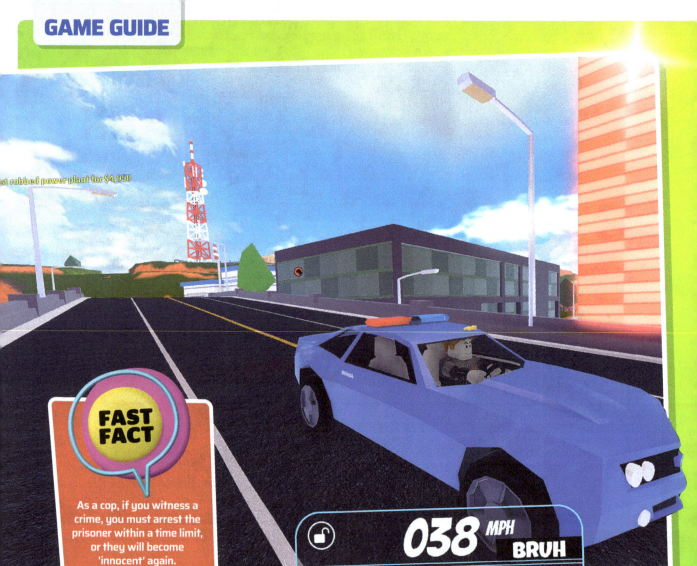

st robbed power plant for $4,950

FAST FACT

As a cop, if you witness a crime, you must arrest the prisoner within a time limit, or they will become 'innocent' again.

038 MPH

BRUH

2 mi

JAILBREAK

Ready to beat the law?

Created in January 2017, Jailbreak quickly rose up the ranks to become one of the platform's most popular games. As the name suggests, it delivers a Roblox version of the classic cops and robbers scenario, where you can choose to become either a criminal or a crime stopper. If you decide to be a criminal, then your ultimate goal is to escape from prison and live a life of crime.

It's up to you what criminal capers you take on: you can rob banks, shops and even trains to get in-game currency, but with every crime you commit, you will accrue a bounty. As a cop, your goal is to guard prisoners and catch any that

escape in order to earn money. The criminals with the highest bounties are displayed at the police stations. Combine this in a multiplayer setting, and you get a seriously enjoyable game.

TOP 5 WEAPONS YOU SHOULD GET

Live to fight another day with these essential firearms

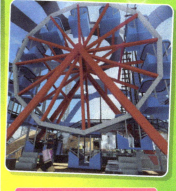

UZI

1 The Uzi is the number one weapon in Jailbreak. The reload time is the second fastest in the game at just 1.333 seconds, and it's tied with the rifle and plasma pistol for the highest fire rate at 750 rounds per minute, which will take out anyone silly enough to challenge you.

SNIPER RIFLE

2 There aren't many things more satisfying than landing a one-shot kill with a sniper rifle. Despite only taking one shot at a time, in the right hands the damage and efficiency of this firearm is too good to pass up. The scope also makes it easy to track enemies from distance.

SHOTGUN

3 Probably one of the best short-range weapons within any Roblox game, a shotgun will obliterate any player that gets in your way. The only downside is that it's pretty woeful at long distances. It's able to deal plenty of damage with a single shot, providing the target is close enough.

ROCKET LAUNCHER

4 A rocket launcher will obliterate anyone from anywhere. There's just one drawback though: using it can take a lot of time, plus you have to purchase the rockets separately. The price may be off-putting, but the damage it does is insane. Rockets deal up to 78 damage – more than three quarters of a player's health.

REVOLVER

5 A revolver deals a health damage of 25 per shot, making it one of the most damaging weapons in the game. It can be gained for free and has a solid reload speed. A four-shot kill at any range (five if including constant health regeneration) is enough to eliminate another player.

QUICK TIPS

LOAD UP
Make sure your weapons are fully loaded when possible. You don't want to pull out your gun and hear the click of humiliation.

LOCK YOUR CAR
Lock your car or it will get stolen, as that's kind of the point of the game. It is possible to walk everywhere, but you'll be left in the dust.

USE THE THIRD-PERSON VIEW
Many Roblox players are comfortable in first-person, since it's similar to games like *Minecraft*, but try zooming out. It can help you avoid being snuck up on.

Images: TrueAnimals

ALSO CHECK OUT

MAD CITY
Cause chaos as a super villain or join the police force and bring justice to the streets – or become a superhero and save the city with your superpowers.

WANTED
As a law enforcer or as a dirty mafioso, with various places to rob or to protect, your job is to earn your place in a city where the chaos never stops.

DAWN OF AURORA
Enter a sci-fi city and rob the Bank of Aurora, or defend and arrest criminals as the defensive military force, FEAR. The choice is yours.

THE TOP FOUR HEIST LOCATIONS

These are the locations to target for the biggest paydays!

BANK

You can't beat a good old-fashioned bank robbery. If you're looking for a showdown with the police, along with some great roleplay scenarios and plenty of awesome rewards, the bank is definitely the place to be. You'll need to walk across a series of obstacles in order to reach the main vault, while keeping an eye out for the police to avoid getting busted. In total, there are eight floors below the bank that need to be tackled.

STATS

Jailbreak has been played

OVER A BILLION TIMES

Each in-game hour is

40 SECONDS LONG

The M12 Molten was the first-ever community-created item in Jailbreak

IT'S WORTH

599,000

IN-GAME CASH

JEWELLERY STORE

The Jewellery Store is one of the most challenging places to pull off a heist, but the rewards are worth the effort. Criminals must smash glass cases, pass through deadly obstacles and dodge laser detectors before parachuting from the roof and delivering the loot to one of the Criminal Bases. The location is a tall, blue building in the Rising City, close to the Rising City Criminal Base. Cops often camp at this locality since it is so easy to rob.

MUSEUM

The Museum is one of the easiest robberies in the game, and one of the most rewarding. Located next to the Radio Tower, it houses plenty of artefacts to swipe, including dinosaur bones and discoveries from Ancient Egypt. The Museum has two vehicle spawn locations: the Boxer is situated on the left of the building, and the Badger is located beside the parking lot. Use one of these to make an escape, should your vehicle be seized during the heist.

POWER PLANT

Once just a regular building, the Power Plant is now an intricate robbery involving the theft of green uranium. To get inside, locate a damaged electricity box near the entrance and solve a logic puzzle that appears on the screen. The puzzle changes at random each time players try to get inside, which makes some heists more challenging than others. The payout depends on how quickly you can transport the uranium to the collectors, so you'll need a fast car.

FAST FACT

As a criminal, you can escape by stealing a helicopter, but it may make it hard to shake off your pursuers.

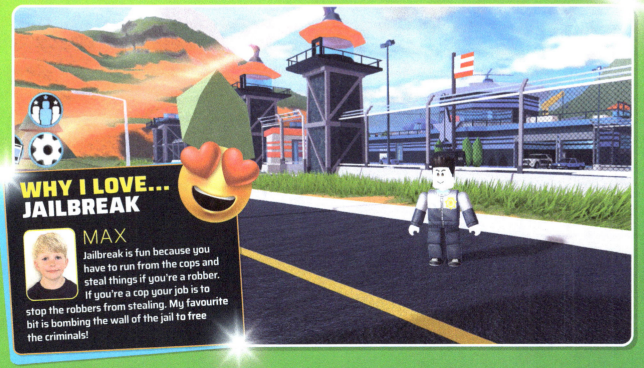

WHY I LOVE...
JAILBREAK

MAX
Jailbreak is fun because you have to run from the cops and steal things if you're a robber. If you're a cop your job is to stop the robbers from stealing. My favourite bit is bombing the wall of the jail to free the criminals!

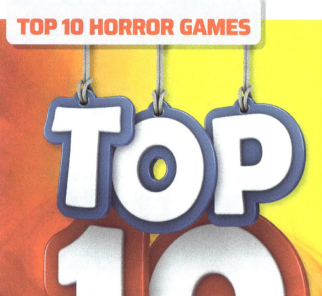

TOP 10

SURVIVAL AND HORROR GAMES

Do you dare to face your fears in these ghoulish games?

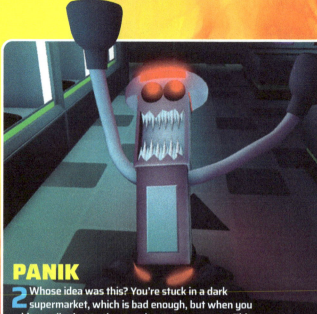

PANIK

2 Whose idea was this? You're stuck in a dark supermarket, which is bad enough, but when you add an evil robot to the map, it gets even worse. This inescapable android has only one thing on its mind: to grab you and turn you into fresh goods at the checkout. Cool cosmetics, alternate maps and a shopping list of items to collect make Panik a blast.

PIGGY

3 There's something uniquely disturbing about a pig that never stops chasing you and turns homicidal if it catches up with you. Like the Terminator, this unfriendly farmyard animal – the Baconator? – can't be reasoned with or defeated; you just have to stay ahead of it. Play Piggy with a bunch of friends and see if you can escape this gammon ghoul.

APEIROPHOBIA

1 Let's kick off with Apeirophobia, which means 'fear of infinity' – a perfect concept for this long, relentless game in which you enter dark rooms at your peril. If you survive the monsters and jump-scares, you'll have to solve puzzles and use your wits to make progress. If you don't like flashing lights and gory scenes, stay away from this one!

DOORS

4 The innocently titled Doors is a horror game with a difference. As well as creeping around a map that will supply you with jump-scares aplenty, you're required to solve puzzles, overcome challenges and use your brain as well as your trigger finger. There's more to Doors than just fear, so try it with headphones on and lights off, if you dare.

RAINBOW FRIENDS

5 Beware that friendly game title: these 'friends' are anything but. You find yourself on a field trip with chums whose smiles soon reveal their evil intentions – how long before these supposed allies become antagonists? Your task is to escape this day out gone wrong in one piece. Play in multiplayer for the best – which is to say, the spookiest – experience.

EVADE

6 One of the most popular Roblox games of all time, even though it's terrifying. You're being stalked by a range of classic figures from popular culture who have metamorphosed into monsters – yes, that really is a zombie SpongeBob. Fight or run if you want to survive – if you're in an evil mood, you can play as one of these villains.

FAST FACT

Loads of horror games on Roblox are inspired by movies, such as *Dead Silence*, based on the 2007 film of the same name.

CHEESE ESCAPE

7 Yes, this does sound ridiculous, and you know what? It is. You're in a world of cheese, where you're being chased by a monstrous rat that is evidently tired of eating cheese all the time, and wants to supplement its diet with you. Run down those long, cheesy corridors or you'll be snapped up.

3008

9 Being stuck in a darkened supermarket was bad enough, but in 3008 you're stuck inside a popular Swedish furniture warehouse that you've probably heard of – now, how grim is that? All sorts of terrible foes await you as you trundle past the lifestyle accessories and meatball stands. Defeat the game by building your own custom area and defending it.

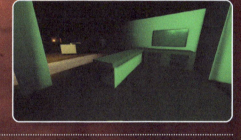

ELMIRA

8 Oh great – another 'school trip gone very badly wrong' experience! This time, you fall asleep on the school bus, and when you wake up, you're the only person left, it's the middle of the night, and you're right outside some sort of terrifying hospital. Much as you might be tempted to quit out at this point, be brave, walk on in and see what awaits you.

8:43

SPIDER

10 You've been chased by a pig and a rat so far – why don't we add a massive spider to the mix? Arachnophobes should probably stay away from this experience, in which a giant eight-legged freak comes after you. Keep running and you'll be fine, though, especially if you invite friends to help. All in all, this is one of the best survival games on the web. Get it?

THREE WAYS TO SURVIVE

Escape the monsters and live to fight another day with these tips!

1 FIGHT SMART
Choose your weapons wisely, assuming any are available. If you're unarmed, run. If you can't, hide. If you can't hide, use your fists. If your enemy is stronger, it's only a game!

2 TEAM UP
Find a multiplayer game if you don't want to endure a horror map alone. Don't trust randoms, though – connect with friends and face your adversaries as a team. It's much safer that way!

3 USE YOUR BRAIN
Study your enemies' weaknesses and exploit them for a better chance of victory. Take a close look at the map, too: which of its features can you use for protection, and which should you avoid? The clever strategist wins the day.

<Marine Fortress>

BLOX FRUITS

Become the pirate king!

Blox Fruits is a pirate adventure game that's based on the iconic *One Piece* anime franchise, and sees players competing against each other to become pirate kings. It's a combat game that takes everything people love about Roblox – community, grinding and exploring – and puts it in one place.

The central concept is to level up your character and earn new powers, which take the form of Blox Fruits. These will give your plucky pirate some serious superpowers. Whether you want to embody a legendary dragon, become one with volcanic magma, or simply summon a magic door with which to

escape, these power-ups are the key to unlocking your pirate's potential.

Like any pirate, you'll need to travel from island to island as you progress through levels. If you don't want to rely on magical powers, you can also become a master swordsman.

TOP **5** BLOX FRUITS

Discover some of the best Blox Fruits to find in-game

BUDDHA FRUIT

1 Considered one of the best Blox Fruits due to its notorious damage-reducing capabilities, Buddha Fruit transforms players into giant Buddhas that inflict a lot of damage. Players can defeat the strongest bosses and complete the toughest raids with Buddha Fruit. You can also travel via sea using this fruit.

FLAME FRUIT

2 Flame Fruit is one of the basic fruits that's available to players, but is extremely powerful thanks to its damage and range potential. Ideal for raids, PvPs and boss fights due to its high knock back and burn damage, Flame Fruit is exceptional for its price, costing only $250,000.

QUICK TIPS

COMPLETE QUESTS

In order to progress through the game and become a pirate king, you must complete quests. Be sure not to take any quests higher than your current level.

GATHER ENEMIES

Instead of killing enemies one by one, you can speed up this process by slowly gathering them at a single spot. Walk close to them, and they will start following you.

ZOOM OUT

If everything looks and feels incredibly huge, you can zoom out. This is helpful when fighting a group of enemies, as you can zoom out and see all of their spawn locations.

LEOPARD FRUIT

3 One of the rarest fruits in the game, Leopard Fruit has a 0.7 percent chance of spawning. Consuming the fruit transforms you into a leopard, greatly increasing your movement and making you immune to lava damage. You also gain two dangerous moves; one melee and one AOE (area of effect).

VENOM FRUIT

4 Venom Fruit is one of the deadliest fruits in the game. The spell showcase of Venom Fruit revolves around causing poisonous damage. Players can also morph into a three-headed hydra and engage in nail-biting battles. This fruit is one of 13 that glow in their physical forms.

Images: Wiki: Limeturtkle; MrGoldyFishy

DOUGH FRUIT

5 One of the best fruits in the entire game, Dough Fruit is known by the community for its strong passive ability, which can help players to stay immune to all physical attacks. With Dough Fruit, you can fight against the most evasive enemies on the map.

ALSO CHECK OUT

KING LEGACY

Like Blox Fruits, King Legacy is inspired by the *One Piece* anime. You can use swords and abilities to battle dangerous foes, while collecting Devil Fruits that give you special powers.

FRUIT BATTLEGROUNDS

If you want something that's easy to pick up and play, Fruit Battlegrounds is one big battleground: perfect if you have an argument to settle.

THE STRONGEST BATTLEGROUNDS

Take part in epic battles, using extraordinary attacks to move the earth. It's easy to get started and hard to put down.

FOUR BEST RAID BOSSES

Discover some of the toughest bosses in Blox Fruits

CAKE QUEEN

With a massive HP of 260,875, Cake Queen is the most powerful Third Sea Boss in the game. Only players with Buddha Devil Fruits and Legendary Swords will have what it takes to defeat her and collect the Buddy Sword, a Legendary sword with a drop rate of five per cent – not to mention 2 million XP. Cake Queen can be found on the second island in the Sea of Treats in the Third Sea, also known as Ice Cream Land.

STATS

THERE ARE 35 BLOX FRUITS

They include 20 Natural Blox Fruits, 10 Elemental Blox Fruits and 5 Beast Blox Fruits.

LEOPARD FRUIT

is the rarest fruit to find.

Including old or removed fruits, it would cost

$54,132,500

TO BUY EVERY FRUIT IN THE GAME. THAT'S SOME SERIOUS COIN!

BEAUTIFUL PIRATE

Beautiful Pirate becomes available once you reach level 1,950. Upon reaching Hydra Island, which is the only area where this Third Sea Boss can be spawned, use long-range attacks and powerful Devil Fruits to defeat him. If successful, players will earn a million XP and 50,000 in-game money and acquire the Cavander, a Legendary sword with a five per cent drop rate. To complete the quest, you must also win against the second form of Beautiful Pirate.

LONGMA

Longma is a level 2,000 boss that uses the infamous Tushita sword. He also has 80,000 HP and does massive AOE damage. You'll find him at the Floating Turtle, behind a door near the Previous Hero, which is only accessible after completing the Torch puzzle in the Third Sea. Upon defeating him, assuming you have inflicted 100 per cent of the damage, he will drop the Legendary sword. You will also receive 50,000 in-game money and the Celestial Swordsman title.

SOUL REAPER

A level 2,100 Raid Boss, Soul Reaper wields Hallow Scythe, one of the five Mythical swords in the game. This Raid Boss also has 260,500 health and administers staggering damage. Deal at least ten per cent damage to Soul Reaper to be guaranteed the Holy Crown and Bones as rewards for defeating him, as well as a five per cent chance of getting the Hallow Scythe. He can be summoned by using a Hallow Essence at the Haunted Castle.

FAST FACT

Electric Claw is the coolest-looking Blox Fruit, as you can literally become Wolverine, but with electricity.

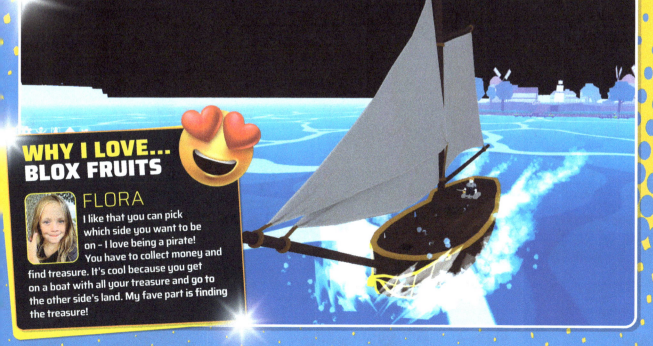

WHY I LOVE... BLOX FRUITS

FLORA

I like that you can pick which side you want to be on – I love being a pirate! You have to collect money and find treasure. It's cool because you get on a boat with all your treasure and go to the other side's land. My fave part is finding the treasure!

TOP 10 BUILDING GAMES

Fancy making money out of construction? Grab your hard hat and let's go

BUILDING SIMULATOR

1 Younger Roblox fans will love this, a cool building game in which you get to construct tanks, houses, towers, castles and more. It's simple to get started and there is a friendly community, so expect to interact with other players. Why not invite your new buddies over for a party?

MINER'S HAVEN

2 You've got an iron and silver mine when your Miner's Haven campaign begins, but why stop there? Your goal is to upgrade your mining empire to include goodies such as rubies and diamonds, but it's not as easy as sticking a shovel in the ground and pulling it out. You'll need a set of conveyor belts, excavators and purifiers, as well as a shop to sell goods.

BUILD A BOAT FOR TREASURE

3 The goal here is simple: design and build a watercraft of your choice, set sail and search for the ultimate artefact – a treasure chest filled with gold. As you drift merrily across the map, the environment will get tougher, so you'll need to upgrade your boat as you go along. You can buy cool boosters such as balloons, weapons and even a jet engine.

WHATEVER FLOATS YOUR BOAT

4 You're on an island. The water level is rising, though, so you'd better assemble the necessary materials for building a ship. Fortunately, they're all right there. Once your watercraft is afloat, it's game on, with other ships engaging you in a series of sea battles. If you master the in-game physics correctly, you'll be able to get your boat to fly – yes, really.

MY RESTAURANT!

5 Build a must-visit place to eat, staff it with friends, invite players over and feed them delicious food! But don't forget to maintain your restaurant, hire a trustworthy crew, keep the kitchen equipment clean, and do all the things that a responsible business owner has to do. Invest in your place to eat, and the customers will line up to see what you have to offer.

BUILD TO SURVIVE

6 Who doesn't remember constructing a fort out of their parents' sofa cushions? Now you can repeat this childhood feat in Build To Survive, where you build a castle and defend it against waves of enemies. These begin with weak mobs that are easily vanquished, but they soon evolve into attacks by truly heinous monsters who will require all your defence expertise.

FAST FACT

Get your construction terms right: 'building' is assembling a structure or device, while 'modelling' is copying something found in the real world.

BUILD IT!

7 If you want a game that gives you plenty of options, look no further. You can compete in Build Battles where you have eight minutes to construct a given structure, after which the winner is voted on. The other option is Free Build, where either alone or with friends, you can construct whatever you imagine.

BUILD YOUR SPACESHIP

8 This cumbersomely named game does exactly what you'd expect. Build a cool spacecraft with a variety of equipment and materials, blast off, and the universe is yours. You'll land on new worlds, gather items and unlock mysteries.

PLANE CRAZY

9 In addition to aeroplanes, you can assemble cars, boats and even rockets. The only condition is that your vehicle must adhere to the laws of physics or it won't budge – not a good look when you're battling other vehicles.

CRAFT A BOAT

10 Sure, you know how to build a boat, right? Wait, you don't? That's okay, because this game will help you to build your first one and get it out on the water. Choose the material types and their shape and launch it on its adventure to see how fast it will travel before sinking. Builds can be saved for future use.

THE RULES OF BUILDING

Three ways that your build might fall foul of the laws of Roblox

⭐1 WATCH YOUR HEIGHT

Build any structure above a certain height on certain maps, and you'll get an error message – for example, the city of Bloxburg permits no more than six levels.

⭐2 ISLAND LIFE

Building on an island? The horizontal build limit is 333 blocks from bedrock, so don't rely on being able to build a bridge to the next chunk of land.

⭐3 DO YOUR RESEARCH

Constructing a plane, boat or other vehicle? Remember, both in-world and physical laws apply to its build and use, so check a tutorial before you begin!

FAST FACT

You can choose from various pets, including dogs, cats, dragons and unicorns, each with unique abilities and characteristics.

PET SIMULATOR

Grow your pet army

Every Pet Simulator X player aspires to collect a variety of pets by breaking piles of gold, chests of gold and diamond clusters to gather resources. With just one pet at the beginning, players can use their resources to purchase pet eggs. These eggs eventually hatch into unique creatures that can be traded with other players or fused together to upgrade them into even cooler animals.

As you progress through the game, you can earn rewards, such as coins and gems that can be used to upgrade pets and purchase items like toys, food and accessories. You can also engage in battles with other players and their pets, participate in quests, and explore different areas of the gaming world.

Pet Simulator was an early trendsetter in the world of pet-collecting games, and with several years of content updates already available, there is no shortage of places to explore and pets to collect.

TOP 5 RAREST PETS

Discover some of Pet Simulator's most sought-after animals!

BLUE BIG MASKOT

1 This is easily one of the rarest and most expensive pets for many reasons. Fans that were hoping to claim one needed to play dress up with their Roblox Avatar and unlock the Dress Up! Achievement. Those that did were rewarded with one of the rarest pets around.

HUBERT CAT

2 While gamers can hatch plenty of other feline friends, Hubert is easily one of the rarest to find. You'll need to befriend an admin that has this particular pet, and hope that they will be willing to trade for something, which is highly unlikely, since this pet is so sought-after.

HUGE GOLDEN EASTER CAT

3 With less than 40 Huge Golden Easter Cats available within the game, this is another one of those pets that most players will never get the chance to own. Those that own one of these particular pets have got something worth a pretty penny, or plenty of diamonds.

RAINBOW HUGE PUMPKIN CAT

4 While the regular Pumpkin Cat is not super rare, the Huge Variants are harder to come by. Featuring the lowest overall hatch rate of any animal in the game (0.00002 per cent), anyone lucky enough to get one of these Cursed Egg Exclusive animals has the rarest hatchable animal currently available.

RAINBOW HUGE SAMURAI BULL

5 Easily the most valuable pet available in Pet Simulator, with an estimated value of 150 trillion Diamonds. It's an incredible amount of diamonds that players will need to obtain to get a chance to own this pet.

QUICK TIPS

TRADE PETS
You don't need to make a huge profit on every trade – simply focus on making small, consistent wins. If you do this repeatedly, the gems will start rolling in!

DON'T BUY GOLDEN EGGS
Golden eggs are far more expensive than their less shiny counterparts. The best way to get some Golden Pets is to buy six normal eggs, hatch them, and convert those pets into a Golden Pet.

CLAIM YOUR RANK REWARD
In Pet Simulator, you get a rank reward every six hours, but this needs to be claimed. The reward gives you both gems and coins. Make sure you claim it every time you log in.

ALSO CHECK OUT

PET STORE TYCOON
Saddle up and take charge of your own virtual pet store. Once a pet gets adopted, you earn coins. You can then buy more pets and fill up your store.

PET LEGENDS
This has you train your companions to brace the adventure into the wild. Work your way up the leaderboard to become a legendary pet owner.

PET ZOO
Construct and build your own zoo as you collect various animals to attract visitors and grow your enclosures. The more visitors at your zoo, the more coins you make.

Get more out of your trading

TOP 10 TIPS

FOR TRADING IN PET SIM

FOCUS ON MYTHICAL PETS

3 Focus on getting a large number of Mythical pets, which you can turn into more valuable Rainbow or Dark Matter pets. You can then trade these pets for Huge pets like a Huge Hell Rock or a Huge Cupcake, which are relatively cheap. Rinse and repeat this process, exchanging these pets for more valuable ones with better enchantments.

UNLOCK THE TRADING PLAZA

1 The Trading Plaza allows you to participate in trade and voice chat. It gives you access to any machine in the game, but you'll need a million diamonds to unlock it. If you don't have enough of them, then mine coins and diamonds in the Spawn World or purchase them with Robux.

USE A VALUE LIST

2 Using a value list is a great way of keeping track of the value of your pets. There are many available online, and while these values are not set in stone, they are helpful in giving you some idea of your pets' worth, which can be used to determine whether a trade is fair or not.

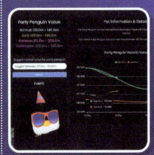

DON'T SERVER HOP

4 When looking for a very specific trade, server-hopping is perhaps necessary, but make sure you spend sufficient time on each server to make sure you aren't missing out. Spending at least ten minutes on each server gives you the best chance of sniffing out a good deal.

STATS

TO MAKE HUGE PETS, YOU WILL NEED TO SPEND

10,000,000

DIAMONDS TO UNLOCK THE HUGE-A-TRON MACHINE

Pet Simulator is one of the most popular Roblox games out there, with

OVER 3 MILLION LIKES

HUGE EASTER CAT

is the rarest huge pet ever released in this game. The chances of hatching this pet are

0.002%

TRADE BOTH PETS AND DIAMONDS

5 You can trade both pets and diamonds via the Pet Simulator trade screen. While newer players will likely be trading pets between each other, high-level players exchange pets for diamonds and vice-versa, with other pets acting like bargaining chips to bring the cost of diamonds down.

TRADE FROM ANYWHERE

6 You can trade absolutely anywhere – you don't even need to be near another player. As long as they're on the same server, the menu will work just fine. Seasoned players can unlock and enter the Trading Plaza behind the eggs in the Spawn World, but it's a means to the same end.

USE ROPRO TO JOIN SERVERS

7 If you have friends playing Pet Simulator, the Roblox client forces you to join their servers by default. Using an extension like RoPro to choose the server you'd like to join makes server-hopping easier and gives you the ability to join more crowded Trade Plazas.

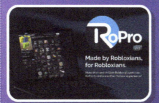

PRIORITISE SMALL WINS

8 You won't usually make an insane profit on any one trade. As such, make sure you prioritise small profits instead of trying to get a ridiculous trade. These small wins will add up if you consistently grind trading. Additionally, remember never to make a value-loss. A demand-loss is fine, but a value-loss is unacceptable.

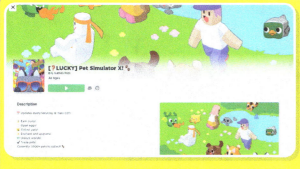

VISIT DIFFERENT LOBBIES

9 Whenever you're in a new lobby, always ask if anybody's interested in your trade. You can soon move to the next one if you can't find any interested parties. Who knows – you might just stumble upon a secret area.

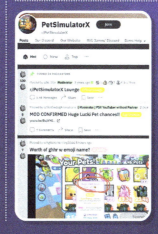

JOIN COMMUNITIES OUTSIDE OF ROBLOX

10 You can also join communities outside of Roblox, such as Discord or Reddit communities, to find people playing the game and see if you can come to a mutual agreement regarding a trade. Just remember that Roblox cannot enforce any deals made between players outside the platform.

WHY I LOVE... PET SIMULATOR

DANIEL

Pet Simulator X is one of my favourite games because I love getting pets and trading them or buying more expensive pets. If you get the best types of pets, called Titanic, you can even ride them. Or you can sell them for more gems or pets. The more gems you own the better pets you can buy. The pets are for breaking coins, chests, presents and crates. My best pet is a 132Q, which can do an enormous amount of damage.

TOP 10 ADVENTURE GAMES

Let's head off to find adventure in these thrill-packed games!

TREASURE QUEST

1 This dungeon-based experience will pit you against many powerful enemies, so make sure you ransack as many treasure chests as possible for improved weapons and cosmetics. A dungeon grind with friends or randoms will enable you to power up fast and embark on fresh campaigns with a full arsenal of defences. By the end of the game, you'll be the master of any underground stronghold.

PIRATE'S TALE

2 Parrot? Check. Three-cornered hat? Check. Barrel of rum? Check. The desire to battle other ships and take all their treasure? Definitely check! As well as these noble pursuits, Pirate's Tale allows you to fight sea monsters, take part in PvP campaigns and explore a huge map. See you there, me hearties.

DRAGON BLADE

3 Inspired by the classic *Legend Of Zelda* games, Dragon Blade takes you deep inside the magical world of Terragonia, where you'll ride atop a dragon (or a horse if you're afraid of heights) and complete many exciting quests. Along the way you can collect armour and weapons and design an entire kingdom. It's an epic adventure alright – just don't fall off that dragon.

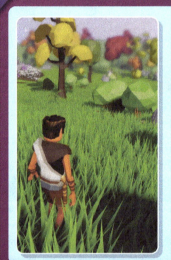

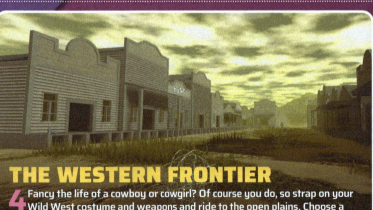

THE WESTERN FRONTIER

4 Fancy the life of a cowboy or cowgirl? Of course you do, so strap on your Wild West costume and weapons and ride to the open plains. Choose a lawful or outlaw path, and make your decisions accordingly: are you going to rob banks or arrest bank-robbers? Along the way there's a ton of quests to complete, so keep your horse watered and your powder dry.

BLOX ADVENTURES

5 What we ideally want from our adventure maps in Roblox is for them to get more challenging and surreal, and that's exactly what happens in Blox Adventures. Not a single world map, but several, it allows you to earn coins and unlock more realms, notably a multiplayer racing mode.

LITTLE WORLD

6 This adventure takes place from the viewpoint of an insect, because you are one! In Little World, your task is to survive the challenges of life as a bug, which isn't easy, because you're at the bottom of the food chain. Get through it by collecting fruit, solving puzzles and metamorphosing into a new animal each time you level up.

Weevolt

Electric

This Electric-type Loomian is often found playing in thunderstorms, where it uses its tail as a lightning rod to gather energy from lightning strikes. It can send powerful jolts of electricity through its whiskers to stun prey.

Choose

LOOMIAN LEGACY

7 If you're into *Pokémon*, you'll love Loomian Legacy. The Loomian creatures aren't exactly like Pikachu and Charmander, of course, but the same sense of fun and community is there. Take them with you on quests, engage in combat against NPCs and collect as many Loomian characters as you can. With over 200 to discover, you'll want to stay all day.

YOUR BIZARRE ADVENTURE

8 If you've seen the *JoJo's Bizarre Adventure* anime, you'll know what to expect. It's packed with surreal characters, and set in a city with secrets and unpredictable plot twists. Defeat enemies, complete quests, create gangs and become the world's most powerful hero.

My dream is to avoid running into security officers with this stolen suitcase!

WINDS OF FORTUNE

9 Build a ship, craft weapons, skill up and explore this excellent, high-seas map for a second stint as a pirate. This time out, your mind will be blown by the stunning graphics and gameplay physics, as well as the ruthlessness of the rival sea-bandits that you'll be up against. Defeat them all, fill the hold with treasure and rule the waves.

FAST FACT

Many Roblox adventure games offer you the choice of free-play or story modes. Because of the high-energy nature of these games, story mode can be exhilarating. Which is your favourite?

VESTERIA

10 The world map of the magical land of Vesteria is both physically beautiful and mentally challenging, so don't be surprised if you find yourself so at home here that you're reluctant to leave. As the hero in an adventure saga, you'll be required to raid citadels, unlock towns, defeat a range of enemies and complete quests – hey, it's the perfect adventure!

BE AN ADVANCED ADVENTURER!

Three ways to enjoy an epic campaign

1 KEEP AN OPEN MIND

You don't always have to be a knight or a pirate. For example, Get A Snack At 3AM is a completely different, but equally challenging, type of adventure.

2 LOVE THE LANDSCAPE

By their nature, adventure games tend to be set in physically expansive and visually thrilling maps. At various points, put your sword or wand down and admire the terrain.

3 BUILD YOUR ARSENAL

Adventure means enemies, so pick up as many defensive weapons as you can. Don't attack NPCs if they're not aggressive; you'll waste resources and energy, as well as putting yourself in needless danger. Focus on the real enemies!

BEDWARS

Not fit for sleepyheads

FAST FACT

Catch a special fish using a fishing rod and you could be rewarded with a rocket launcher and 12 rockets.

Consistently ranked as one of the most popular games on Roblox, the objective of BedWars is to destroy other player's beds while protecting your own. If your base gets destroyed, your death in the game becomes permanent and the last player surviving becomes the ultimate winner. It's an easy enough concept, but don't go underestimating it!

There's a huge variety of weapons, including vehicles to attack the enemy's sleeping quarters. Go it alone or team up with other players at war to protect their own king-size. The game also features other popular multiplayer modes from *Minecraft*, including SkyWars and Lucky Blocks.

There are enchantments and several unique kits that provide their own perks and bonuses when equipped – so if building bases and lolloping between waves of mobs is your go-to activity, then you're sure to feel at home with BedWars.

TOP 5 KITS

Discover BedWars' best kits and their special abilities

GRIM REAPER

1 This is the best kit in BedWars Roblox for aggressive players who like to engage in close combat, as it allows you to safely escape fights by consuming the souls of dead enemies. The soul provides increased speed, invulnerability and health regeneration for 2.5 seconds.

MELODY

2 Melody is the best support kit in the game, as it uses a guitar and the power of music to heal teammates. It is essential for one member of your team to have this kit, especially beginners. You can purchase a guitar from the item store for 20 iron bars.

ELDERTREE

3 This kit is best for passive players who like to prepare for the late game. It lets you collect tree orbs across the map to increase both your physical size and maximum HP. However, you cannot equip any armour in the early parts of the game.

BARBARIAN

4 Barbarian has a feature called Rage Mode that allows you to build rage by damaging enemies in order to upgrade your sword. Damaging your enemies will fill the rage meter, which automatically upgrades your current sword on completion of the meter.

ARCHER

5 The Archer is the perfect kit for players who like to fight from long range, as it provides 15 per cent more damage while using projectiles like bows and arrows. Players can also buy an exclusive tactical crossbow from the item shop for eight emeralds.

QUICK TIPS

GAIN A HEIGHT ADVANTAGE

A 1v1 is usually decided based on who gets the first hit. Having blocks will give you a height advantage via quick building.

RUSH YOUR NEIGHBOUR

Getting rid of your neighbour gives you access to two generators, doubling your income and allowing you to get your items faster.

LEARN HOW TO GEN SPLIT

Every BedWars player should know how to Gen Split. It allows multiple players to receive the same iron simultaneously.

ALSO CHECK OUT

SKYWARS

Build, connect and fight to hold your position. If you've spent time mopping up the BedWars servers, then you'll have an idea of how SkyWars works, too.

ISLANDS

Islands takes a lot of *Minecraft* ingredients and gives them a *Roblox* twist. The idea is mostly the same: take a floating island and transform it into a bustling community hub.

TOWER DEFENSE SIMULATOR

Earn coins to expand your defences, but instead of going toe-to-toe with opposing players, work alongside them to fend off waves of zombies.

TOP 10 WEAPONS

You'll need the best weapons to wreck your opponents' beds

ICE SWORD

3 The Ice Sword can only be purchased by Freiya kit users and replaces the Emerald Sword in the item shop as a kit-exclusive melee weapon. The sword increases the duration of Freiya's Frost ability from 1.6 seconds to 2.5 seconds, as well as inflicting 47 attack damage. Players lose this weapon when they die.

RAGEBLADE

4 Rageblade is a Barbarian-only weapon. Whenever a player with a Barbarian kit reaches their maximum level of wrath, their sword is transformed into a Rageblade. The Rageblade inflicts 65 attack damage with a cooldown time of 0.3 seconds. If that player dies, half of their rage will be lost.

ROCKET LAUNCHER

1 The Rocket Launcher inflicts the most damage out of any weapon in the game and is capable of killing multiple players at once. It fires a rocket that bursts in front of players, doing AOE damage and demolishing nearby blocks. Six rockets, along with a rocket launcher, can be obtained by breaking a lucky block.

GOLDEN SCYTHE

2 The Golden Scythe is a melee weapon and can only be found in lucky blocks and lucky airdrops. When attacking enemy players it deals 70 damage per hit. It's tied with the Rageblade for the third best damage per hit of all melee weapons, behind the Twirlblade and the Baseball Bat.

CARROT CANNON

5 Carrot Cannon is a weapon that covers a wide area. Using vending machines is the only way to get one. When loaded with carrot rockets, they can fire a burst of four rockets at once, causing up to 60 damage to adjacent foes and blocks.

STATS

MOST CONTESTS LAST

20-30 minutes

THERE ARE

4 CLASSIC GAME MODES

SHOP KITS COST

399 ROBUX EACH

FAST FACT

The big wood sword is currently the biggest sword in the game. It can only be obtained as a drop from lucky blocks.

RED HYPER LASER GUN

6 This gun's description states that the Red laser is the fastest colour laser. Seeing it in action, that's probably true. It's not a bad weapon to get if you're looking to end things quickly and with minimal fuss: clean, effective and red. What more can you ask for?

HISTORIC 'TIMMY' GUN

7 The Historic 'Timmy' Gun is known for its compactness, reliability, ergonomics and a high volume of automatic fire. Modelled after the Thompson 'Tommy' sub-machine gun, you will feel like Al Capone.

MARSHMALLOW SHOOTER

8 The Marshmallow Shooter does exactly what you would expect: shoot marshmallows. Undoubtedly, this gun has limited combat effectiveness, but players can use it to shoot toasty treats at their team members. The idea of being hit by a marshmallow and sustaining damage is priceless.

XLS MARK II PULSE LASER PISTOL

9 This science-fiction-inspired gun dons the appearance of a weapon used by futuristic humans. It actually looks like something Marvin the Martian would use, but don't be fooled; it will disintegrate anyone unfortunate enough to be on the receiving end of it. Grab one to both dazzle and annihilate simultaneously.

LUGER PISTOL

10 The iconic Luger Pistol is at number 10. Modelled after the iconic German pistol, it's an old-school relic that allows players to reap multiple benefits. Shooting an opponent in the leg with this pistol will deal significant damage and drastically reduce their running speed.

FAST FACT

The most popular kit is the builder kit, which provides a wooden pickaxe, bricks of wool, blocks of glass, endstone blocks and blocks of obsidian.

WHY I LOVE... BEDWARS

SAMMIE

BedWars is a great PVP game and perfect for fans of *Minecraft*. There are loads of game modes to play, such as Doubles, SkyWars, 30v30, Squads, Lucky Block and many more! I love BedWars because it's a great game to play with my friends!

TOP 10 COMBAT GAMES

Fancy yourself as a king's champion or ninja warrior?

NINJA LEGENDS

1 Since its launch, Ninja Legends has enjoyed over a billion visits. With a range of combat moves, as well as attractive upgrades, cool characters, cute pets and new locations, it's an incredible map. Don't worry if you know nothing about martial arts: learn a few moves and you'll be on your way to mastery.

N THE JOJO GAME

2 Any guesses which TV franchise influenced this game? Yes, it's the mighty *JoJo's Bizarre Adventure*, with all the surreal dialogue and over-the-top action sequences that the popular title suggests. It's not what you'd call a true-to-life game, with hilariously exaggerated physics and a unique aesthetic, but when was that ever a problem for us Robloxers?

ANIME FIGHTER SIMULATOR

3 Ever wanted to fight as a character from your favourite anime? Of course you have! This game allows you to pick from a range of famous animated avatars from the world of film and gaming, and even blend them together to form one super-avatar, before stepping into the combat zone. Multiple worlds and plenty of time-trial minigames add value.

SUPER POWER FIGHTING SIMULATOR

4 As you might guess, this lets you boost your fighting skills. You'll encounter chests, quests and bounties, undergo transformations and even access VIP servers.

SELL

PACKS

PETS

TRADE

FAST FACT

You already know that the most common attack moves in Roblox are punching and kicking, but did you know that parrying is an effective defence stratagem?

SUPER SAIYAN SIMULATOR 2

5 If you're a fan of the *Dragon Ball* franchise, then get straight to Super Saiyan Simulator 2, which places you directly in the *DB* world. It focuses more on combat action than beautiful aesthetics, but there are lots of other landscape-based games if that's not for you.

PILFERING PIRATES

6 Here's a multiplayer fighting game between four pirate ships at the same time, all of which can't stand the other three and want them to head down to Davy Jones's locker as soon as humanly possible. Use cannons to disable the other three craft, then board them and use hand-to-hand combat to overpower the crew and steal their treasure.

ANIME BATTLE ARENA

7 Characters that anime fans worldwide are bound to recognise – *One Piece*'s Luffy, Goku from *Dragon Ball* and a few familiar faces from *JoJo's Bizarre Adventure* – all appear during Anime Battle Arena. For that reason, as well as the fact that the combat moves are both complex and satisfying, you'll have a great time here.

DEMON TOWER DEFENSE

8 This fighting game is inspired by the *Demon Slayer* anime and features waves of unholy enemies, all of whom have a single objective: to overwhelm your tower. As the siege gets more intense, use your stockpile of weapons: if you run out, they'll have your head on a pike!

BOXING LEAGUE

9 Punch, kick, grapple and push your enemies until they surrender. You can customise the experience by boosting XP and choosing from a range of cosmetic options, but essentially this is about hand-to-hand combat.

BLEEDING BLADES

10 Most combat games allow you to control a single character. Others enable you to command an army. Well, Bleeding Blades lets you do both! It's an ancient history-themed campaign, hosting three events: the Battle of Thermopylae, the Siege of Halicarnassus and the Battle of Milvian Bridge. Romans, Greeks and other powers are the forces to deploy.

THREE EFFECTIVE COMBAT TIPS

Live to fight another day with these essential pieces of advice

1 CLEVER CAMERA
Keep your field of view angled so that you can see the sky, or at least most of it. That way, you can detect projectiles and flying mobs in good time, as well as ground-based assaults.

2 PICK THE RIGHT WEAPONS
A sword won't deflect rockets and is no use against someone with a bigger or better sword. Your best bet is to have both a hand-to-hand and ranged weapon, such as a rifle.

3 STUDY INCOMING MOBS
Consider your enemies' assets. You might want to attack the weakest threats to thin out the herd, or take down the quickest attackers to buy some time. Either way, don't just attack indiscriminately or you'll soon be toast!

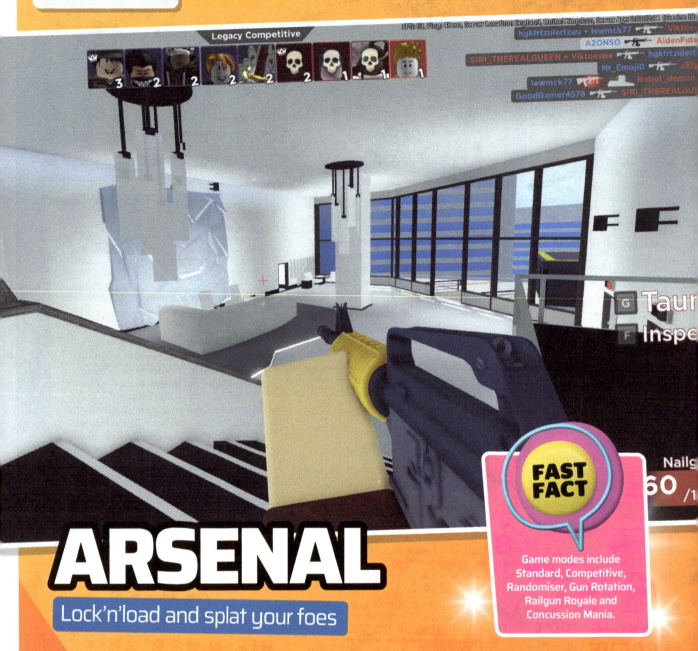

ARSENAL

Lock'n'load and splat your foes

FAST FACT

Game modes include Standard, Competitive, Randomiser, Gun Rotation, Railgun Royale and Concussion Mania.

Arsenal is a Loadout-based game in which you go through a series of diverse weapons with the aim of killing the most players. It's one of the few shooting Roblox games that awards you for being creative, with the use of blades, spells and other weapons to kill your enemies.

In-game, you level up and gain more experience as you obtain more kills. Later, you become richer and can buy weapons, melee items and character skins. In each round, players must get kills or assists and eventually reach 32 kills: the 31st kill is with a golden gun, and the 32nd and final kill is with a golden knife. Both turn the victim into a solid gold statue in the pose they were in when killed. The absence of storyline or quests make this a great game to unwind – no need for fancy tactics or strategy. Only the most adaptable players and skilled shooters will survive.

TOP 5 SKINS

Discover Arsenal's best skins and their special abilities

The Brickbattle and the Retro Zombie skin is an 'Old Roblox'-themed character. It is also the only skin to have the Legendary-Old rarity.

SNAKE EATER

1 It's a challenge to find a more fitting character for Roblox Arsenal than one from *Metal Gear*. 'Snake Eater' refers to US Special Forces veterans – the nickname was earned by the forces serving snake meat to visitors at Fort Bragg.

MATERIAL MAN

2 As dense as a brick wall, the value of the Material Man skin comes from it being able to hide where the player is looking from a quick glance. It can also be a challenge to line up headshots against this skin, as it all looks exactly the same.

CASTLERS

3 Error messages and text typed across its arms and legs make this a confusing skin to wear, but it ranks among our favourites thanks to its sheer oddity. It's one of the rarest skins in the game, and the best way to unlock it is to complete as many matches as possible.

QUICK TIPS

GRAB HEALTH AFTER AN ELIMINATION

The key to surviving after a fight is to pick up the green bottle that drops from the enemy. This will help get you in fighting shape.

KNOW THE SPAWN LOCATIONS

The path to victory is knowing the spawn locations of each map. If you know where a spawn location is, you can run there and find someone to eliminate.

ASSISTS COUNT

Most assisted eliminations count just as much as a solo one does, so if you do damage to a player and your team-mate finishes them off, you will still get credit.

JOE

4 You'll stick out like a sore thumb in this Lego-like character skin. This can work in your favour, as it allows allies to easily find you, and it can attract a good variety of enemies to your position. It's ideal if you like being the centre of attention during a fight.

INVISIBLE MAN

5 This skin isn't entirely honest, as players with this skin aren't invisible. The fedora and sunglasses still offer an imposing look, so you can send your opponents to the afterlife in style while you're using a guitar to blast them away. This skin looks better on the red or green team.

ALSO CHECK OUT

BAD BUSINESS

Bad Business is Roblox's answer to *Call Of Duty* . You can take out every other player in Free For All, or join up with your team in Team Deathmatch.

RECOIL

Shoot your way through maps and get as many kills as possible. This is a fast-paced FPS game where you need the best load-outs to shoot faster than your opponents.

BIG PAINTBALL

With five different maps and game modes to choose from, BIG Paintball promises an action-packed experience with a ton of content. The game also contains over 30 different guns.

TOP 10 GAME MODES

Extra game modes include new weapon restrictions

HARD MODE

2 Hard Mode also requires 16 kills to win using some of the most disliked weapons in the game. The final four weapons in order to win are Golden Gun, Golden Bow, Golden Bomb and Golden Knife. Getting knifed demotes players to the first level. The Golden Bow can also demote players back to the first weapon.

INSANE MODE

3 Insane Mode is similar to Hard, featuring some of the most difficult weapons. Players will have to earn 32 kills, with the final six being Golden Gun, Golden Bow, Golden Hush Puppy, Golden Bomb, Golden Musket and Golden Knife.

PISTOLS

1 This game mode sees battle limited to the Hush Puppy, Dual Volcanics and anything else that's classified as a pistol. The Golden Knife was originally the final weapon to win the round, but has since been removed. The number of kills required to win are reduced to 16, with the Golden Gun being the final weapon.

STATS

THERE ARE CURRENTLY

65 PLAYABLE MAPS

ARSENAL CURRENTLY HAS OVER

13,000

active players

The **paintball gun** has a fast fire rate and infinite ammo, but a low magazine capacity of

20

LASER TAG

4 In this mode, you must rely on nine laser-related weapons: the Laser Rifle, the R800 Railgun, the Handcannon, the Pulse Laser, the Z80, the Focus, the BH10, the Pathbringer and the Pulse Musket. You need 32 kills to win, and the last two need to come via the Golden Gun and the Golden Knife.

FAST FACT

The Pulse Laser has the fastest fire-rate in the game. It also has no spread or recoil.

RANDOMIZER

5 Get placed in a team and receive a different weapon each time you respawn. This game mode lasts for four minutes and the player with the most kills wins. Each kill will reward you with points. Only the Golden Gun can be obtained, but it will not grant you the Golden Knife on a kill.

CONCUSSION MANIA

6 Concussion Mania is a non-standard mode that only utilises the Concussion Rifle. The Golden Knife and Golden Gun are excluded, and the kills required to win are reduced to 16.

STANDARD

7 Arsenal's core gameplay includes all the game's weapons. Each elimination or assist will give you a new one. Standard mode does not end until you get a kill with the Golden Knife in Level 32. Reach it for a final elimination to win!

GUN ROTATION

8 Guns cycle every 20 seconds, with players getting the same random gun until they reach 30 kills. You need 32 to win, ending with the Golden Gun and the Golden Knife.

LEGACY COMPETITIVE

9 Only 31 kills are required to win. There are multiple acceptable weapons and getting a kill with the Golden Gun gives you the win, skipping the Golden Knife. Point and click – it's that easy!

RAILGUN ROYALE

10 In this game mode, you only use the Railgun, which is a handheld, high-velocity weapon that's extremely powerful. It deals 100 body damage and will always instantly kill an enemy, no matter where they are hit on the body. The Golden Gun is the final weapon.

WHY I LOVE... ARSENAL

HECTOR

What I love most about Arsenal is that it is a first-person shooting game with teams and a variety of fun, crazy and wacky guns! You can play all sorts of maps and each is unique in its own way. There are also lots of different things to buy and use.

TOP 10

CRAZY GAMES

Looking for a truly weird Roblox experience? Look no further!

ZOMBIES ARE ATTACKING RODONALDS

1 While other Roblox games feature waves of enemies besieging a castle or fortress, this one has zombies attacking a branch of a famous fast-food chain (the game previously used the McDonald's name before opting for RoDonalds). Make sure your restaurant is secure, or you'll soon be a Big Mac for the undead.

THE PRESENTATION EXPERIENCE

2 A fellow student has to make a presentation on a random subject, and you have one job: distract the teacher. You get points for every five seconds that you create havoc. If only real school was this funny.

HUMAN GIRAFFE

3 Yes, this one is truly odd: it's a game based on what life would be like if you had a long, bendy neck rather like that of a giraffe. Unlike that noble beast, though, your extended neck can be curved into all sorts of shapes, and you're also supplied with a long tongue that can grab onto various objects on the map. Who came up with this idea?

WACKY WIZARDS

4 Far from 'serious' magic or spells that actually benefit a player in some way, the wizardry unleashed in this game ranges from the surreal to the stupid. Throw items such as a brain or a decaying lump of food into a pot, and use the resulting elixir to make yourself shrink, stretch or transform into a frog. Well, why not?

EG-TESTING

5 Transform into an egg, have a few drinks so that you can't walk, or roll, straight, then try to collect money to upgrade the cosmetics of your egg-vatar. It provides a genuinely unusual Roblox experience, if also one that we probably wouldn't play more than once.

SURVIVE ARIANA GRANDE IN AREA 51

6 You can imagine the conversation between this game's developers: "Hey, we should set a game inside the secret military zone, Area 51!" "Great idea. Which enemy mobs shall we use to attack the player?" "How about a modern pop and R&B singer?" Yes, you'll need to fight a swarm of evil Ariana Grandes to survive this game. Don't ask us why.

CHIPOTLE BURRITO BUILDER

7 Chipotle is the name of a Mexican dish, as well as that of an American fast-food chain, with branches in the UK and Europe, and this game is their official corporate experience. While the game is mildly entertaining and allows you to get your hands on some interesting cuisine, the fact that a company's marketing department is guiding you around just feels weird.

DANCING PARROTS

8 Who doesn't enjoy the sight of tropical birds sitting on a branch and shaking a leg to pop tunes and generally having a great day? After an hour or two of this, however, you may realise that your player is unable to move, and unable to shift perspective from the partying avians. It's like you're stuck in parrot purgatory – forever.

WALMART LAND

9 This is the official Walmart Roblox game. While the company is obviously pushing for some sort of fun, Metaverse-style environment for its users, what we actually have is a surreal wander through a load of toys and other store goods. It's hard to see what the point of this game is. Why not go to the actual bricks-and-mortar stores instead?

FAST FACT

From Nike to Gucci to Apple and beyond, Roblox now boasts a ton of official company games. Some are great, others less so, but remember, they're all selling something!

SURVIVE THE PEPPA PIG

10 Now you've got the *Peppa Pig* theme running through your head, haven't you? That's not the only running associated with this game: you'll be sprinting for your life in this game, trying to escape the evil Peppa and her baseball bat. Let's hope these developers never adapt Sonic The Hedgehog into a villain, or we'll all be doomed in five seconds flat.

DESIGN A CRAZY MAP!

Thinking of surprising players with a weird game? Read our top tips...

1  **THINK OUTSIDE THE BOX**

For a surreal experience, set your map somewhere unexpected, like an underwater school, a supermarket in the clouds or a farm on a mountain.

2 **SUPPLY UNEXPECTED GAMEPLAY**

Suppose the biggest boss in your game is a talking rainbow? How about mobs that turn into ice cream when you fight them? Be inventive, and users will thank you for it.

3  **USE REAL-WORLD INSPIRATION**

Don't be afraid to look to real life for game-building ideas. What Roblox does best is add a cool twist to real-world settings – that's why we love it.

Kitsune

Cerberus

Axolotl

ADOPT ME!

Build your pet collection here

If you're interested in building your collection of pets, the first place you should try on Roblox is Adopt Me!, one of the most popular pet games on the platform. With billions of visits reported and millions of users, the experience offers you the chance to buy, trade or adopt a multitude of cute – and not so cute! – animals.

Pets are divided into five divisions, based on their cost and rarity: Common, Uncommon, Rare, Ultra-Rare and Legendary. They hatch from eggs as Newborns, pass through the stages of Juniors, Pre-Teens, Teens and Post-Teens, and ultimately become Full-Grown. You can then merge four of them into a Neon pet, and then merge four Neons into a Mega-Neon animal.

Once you have acquired a pet, remember that your job is to look after it and keep it happy and healthy, so think twice before you lay out Robux on your tenth cat or 20th chinchilla...

Cat
Junior

TOP 5 PET STAGES

Discover what to expect from your pets as they grow

NEWBORN AND JUNIOR

1 The cutest age groups, if you ask us! Hatch your pets and equip their room with a crib, feeder, bath and musical instrument. This means that you can complete tasks such as hygiene, feeding and entertainment in a single room and level up quickly.

PRE-TEEN, TEEN AND POST-TEEN

2 This is where the number of tasks ramps up from 11 for a Common Pre-Teen pet to 62 for a Legendary Post-Teen animal. Grind through these as efficiently as possible with time-saving strategies such as keeping a sandwich on you at all times. This way, you can complete a feeding task as quickly as possible.

FULL-GROWN

3 Your pet has now passed into adulthood with a full set of grown-up behaviours and dimensions. You can keep your cute buddy at this stage if you like: they'll look great and be perfectly happy. Still, their ultimate objective is to turn Neon, so if you have the time for all those tasks, why not help them get there?

NEON

4 Once your pet has reached Neon status, their visuals will blow your mind! They are: Reborn (Newborn), Twinkle (Junior), Sparkle (Pre-Teen), Flare (Teen), Sunshine (Post-Teen) and Luminous (Full Grown). Once you have a bunch of these glittering pets, you'll be the envy of the map.

MEGA-NEON

5 How can you tell if your pet is Neon or Mega-Neon? Once your pets reach this nirvana-like status of evolution, different parts of their anatomies will glow neon, depending on their species. With a herd of luminescent friends accompanying you, you can rest in the knowledge that you've reached Adopt Me!'s ultimate goal.

QUICK TIPS

TIME TO WORK
Prioritise food and water Tasks, and complete them as quickly as you can, because Adopt Me! may randomly assign you another similar Task if you do them fast enough.

MOVE AT SPEED
Use a grappling hook or a magic door to get around the map more quickly. The latter allows you to teleport to your house, making home-based jobs such as the Dirty Task faster to complete.

STOCK UP
Buy pizza dough and store it in your kitchen, so if your Task is to feed yourself or your pet, you can get it nailed fast. Pizza dough is available from the furniture list, oddly enough.

ALSO CHECK OUT

BLOXTOPIA
This RPG game has enjoyed billions of visits since its launch in 2020, and allows you to adopt and raise cute babies and build a home of your choice for them.

OVERLOOK BAY
Build your collection of pets, house them in your own dream home and explore the beautiful world of Overlook Bay, collecting gems and meeting new friends along the way.

BABY CITY
Adopt a baby, explore the map and enjoy a family RPG with friends, this game's bonus element being that you can play with up to 20 friends or randoms here.

FOUR PETS TO COLLECT

Can you collect these cute (and not so cute) animals?

SHADOW DRAGON

1 Is there any cooler pet than a dragon? Heck no, and the Adopt Me! devs know this all too well, introducing a bunch of these fiery lizards to the map. Our favourite is the highly sought-after Shadow Dragon, which comes equipped with a useful Shadow Breath trick and can merge into Neon and Mega-Neon versions if you collect enough of them. There are also variants such as the Bat and Frost Dragons to add to your mythical menagerie.

FAST FACT

For April Fool's Day in 2020, a pet rock was introduced for players who prefer their animals to be quiet and easily manageable.

STATS

ADOPT ME! AVERAGED

160,000 simultaneous players in September 2022. That's a lot of server bandwidth!

OVER **30** BILLION visits

that's more than four visits for every person on the planet.

The developers behind the game, Uplift Studios, apparently earn **$60 MILLION A YEAR FROM IT**

LLAMA

2 When the Farm Egg was updated in November 2019, players could invest 750 in-game cash for a 15 per cent chance of hatching a llama. It's a cool, relaxed pet that is happy to chill out with its owner, but can be persuaded to break out into a little dance once it's fully grown. The Mega Neon version is a pet to show off with its neon chroma visuals, but merging enough Llamas to make one will be quite a feat, as they're so rare.

GIRAFFE

3 Neck and neck (ho ho) with Dragons as Adopt Me!'s coolest pet is the Giraffe, a limited-edition animal that launched in 2019 from the now-unavailable Safari Egg. If you have one of these Eggs, which you can now acquire through trading if you're lucky, you have a three per cent chance of hatching a Giraffe. If you do get one, you'll enjoy its bright colours in Neon and Mega-Neon versions – and the dance trick that unlocks when it reaches adult status.

FAST FACT

Two players called Bethink and NewFissy came up with the idea for Adopt Me! in 2017. Six years later, a team of 40 people manages it.

MONKEY KING

4 To bag yourself this cheeky Monkey King, acquire a regular Monkey and a Premium Monkey Box – the former is a much easier acquisition than the latter. Unbox it with 195 Robux and add three Staff Ingredients, and you can craft yourself a Monkey King, smartly decked out in red and gold armour and equipped with a staff for combat. He can perform two tricks with this staff, making him hugely valuable as a trading item. That said, who could let go of this cute anthropoid?

WHY I LOVE... ADOPT ME!

IZZY

There are so many enjoyable things to do so you can never get bored, such as being a hairdresser for dogs, working at a pizza place, adopting pets, trading, decorating your home and so much more. Weekly updates and daily rewards also make you want to keep playing. It's a great game for making friends and having fun with your friends in real life!

TOP 10

TYCOON GAMES

Stuff your bank account with Robux with these essential tycoon experiences

MEGA MANSION TYCOON

2 Which self-respecting tycoon doesn't have at least one mansion to live in? Build a luxury residence of your own in Mega Mansion Tycoon and equip it with everything you need. These can include massive TV screens, ornate furnishings, chandeliers, huge beds, a fitness room, a home cinema, and, of course, a garage for your fleet of vehicles.

MALL TYCOON

1 Let's start with an easy way to make money: design, build and run a shopping mall. Your objective is to create the best mall on the server, with the coolest stores and the most attractive amenities, so that players will flood in and buy your stuff. Keep it looking nice, redecorate regularly and add up to 12 floors. There'll be no stopping the shopping!

PRISON TYCOON

3 If the idea of running a prison sounds difficult and dangerous, that's because it is – but in Prison Tycoon, the goal is not simply to keep your inmates fed, housed and safe. No, this prison population is your own private army! Once you've built up enough cash and weapons, you can secure your facility with walls, fences and generators, and head out to start building an empire.

HOSPITAL TYCOON

4 Build yourself a luxury medical facility that caters for the health of friends and randoms, and you'll soon be in the money. Unlock new rooms and equipment, add custom cosmetics and build your hospital so that it's as efficient as it can be. There's no real competition in this game; it's all about developing the best healthcare facility that you can.

ZOMBIE MERGE TYCOON

5 The 'Zombie' part of the title is understandable – you'll be managing a herd of zombies, and wreaking havoc as you go. But what about the 'Merge' bit? Well, this means you can blend the undead together to make super-powerful zombie soldiers. Along the way, you'll earn access to increasingly powerful weapons, from a crowbar to a machine gun, to take down yet more zombies.

CAR DEALERSHIP TYCOON

6 Never mind superheroes or armies of undead warriors: this game allows you to buy and sell second-hand vehicles. Perhaps the experience isn't as thrilling as storming a fortress with a broadsword or battling pirates on the high seas, but if you want to learn about changing tyres and giving a new Ford SUV an MOT test, there's nowhere better to go.

ULTRA POWER TYCOON

7 In this case, the 'Power' in Ultra Power Tycoon doesn't mean fiscal power – no, it's all about developing actual physical and/or mental superpowers in an army of heroes. Train your team, give them the skills they'll need to do your bidding, and send them out to do battle with other players' gangs of superhumans. Victory will soon be yours!

GYM TYCOON

8 Not only is Gym Tycoon about building up reserves of cash, it's also about building up your muscles. Lift weights, get ripped, pose in the mirror and then go and do some work in your gym office, where business matters need your attention. The more you work out, the more you'll earn, so don't be lazy – go and do some bench presses!

YOUTUBER TYCOON

9 Becoming a rich and famous online content creator in the real world requires expertise, equipment, time and effort, all so that people can troll you in the comments section – so why not take the Roblox equivalent and become a successful YouTuber the painless way? Earn cash through gaining subscriptions, build a home studio and interact with other creators right here.

PLAYER COMPUTER TYCOON

10 This team-based experience is a little different from most tycoon games. Work with your colleagues on building the best computers that you can, which you can use to earn cash and other rewards. You'll start with an old CRT monitor and half-functioning keyboard, but you'll soon graduate to a state-of-the-art machine with triple screens and a gamer chair.

TOP TYCOON TIPS

The best ways to make money as a Roblox tycoon

★1 WATCH YOUR SPENDING

Roblox will accept as much real-world cash as you care to invest. But beware: overspending in the real and online worlds can be equally catastrophic.

★2 BE INNOVATIVE

What can you bring to your Roblox business that doesn't already exist? Think outside the box and don't simply take the fastest route; there might be better ways to achieve your goals that aren't immediately obvious.

★3 PUT IN THE HOURS

You'll need to work hard to make your vision a reality, so make sure you spend sufficient time running your business. At the same time, take breaks, stay hydrated and turn off your screens for most of your day. You need exercise, fresh air and good nutrition in the real world!

CREATE YOUR OWN ROBLOX GAME!

Looking for true Roblox mastery? Then it's time to create your very own game!

You've played a few games on Roblox, seen a few glitches, had a few experiences that could have been better – and you've said, 'I could make a better game than this!' It sounds like you're ready for the Roblox Studio experience: a chance to create your own gaming experiences and get paid for it. Well, you're in luck: Roblox Studio will pay you around 29 real-world cents for every in-experience dollar that players spend in your game, which may not be quite as good as 100 cents per dollar, but they're giving you free tools and hosting your game at very little cost. What's the downside? If you can handle a bit of simple coding and you have a decent imagination, your game-designing career begins right here.

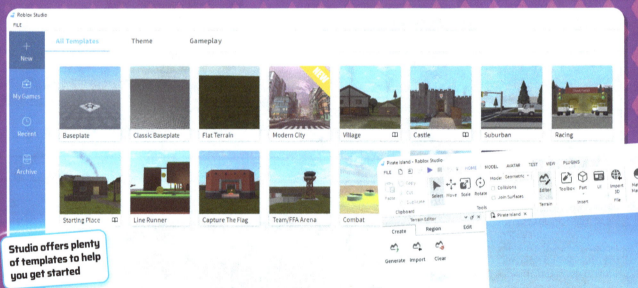

Studio offers plenty of templates to help you get started

LET'S GET STARTED!

Just as you did with the main Roblox game, you can download Roblox Studio onto your PC or Mac computer (it doesn't work on phones yet, sorry!) by going to www.roblox.com and clicking Create > Start Creating > Download and following the prompts. Once installation is complete, open Roblox Studio and you can start creating games, characters, environments and even entire virtual worlds. If you're under 13, always ask parental or guardian permission before downloading and running this or any other program.

The first thing you'll see in Roblox Studio is a + symbol: click this to open a new blank game canvas. Alternatively, you can open a pre-made game template such as a battle arena, a racing game, an obby course, an endless running game and so on, or a pre-made game stage. These include towns, suburbs, cities, villages, castles and islands.

FAST FACT

The very first game released on Roblox Studio is thought to be Rocket Arena, launched (ahem) back in 2006.

BUILDING OBJECTS LIKE A BOSS

Populating a game map is basically about importing objects, editing them and placing them so that they form buildings, machines, environment and other features of the landscape. The first part – importing objects – couldn't be easier: type the name of the item you want, such as 'tree', 'brick', 'car' and so on, into the search bar, and click on it or drag it to import it into your game or stage.

Once the object is there, it's ready for you to do things to it. Click the Home or Model tab at the top of the screen: this will reveal tools called Select, Move, Scale and Rotate. Select your object with the Select tool (a mouse symbol) and a blue boundary box will surround it. Click and drag to move it around the stage.

If you want to delete it, select it and press the Delete key; if you want to move it along one of three red, green and blue axes, use the Move tool (a cross); and to scale it up or down, use the Scale tool (which resembles two nested boxes). Similar tools for rotating, cutting, copying and pasting your object are also available,

and there's even Negate, Union and Separate tools to hollow objects out, fuse and detach them to and from each other. Before you know it, you'll have a map populated with cool objects.

If you want to create a new object from scratch, you have four possible blocks to choose from, edit and combine: get them from the Part menu. Choose from a cuboid Block, a ball-shaped Sphere, an inclined-block Wedge and a pole-shaped Cylinder. Craft them with the tools mentioned above, edit their colours, light effects and materials, and soon you'll have a massive range of shaped objects – enough for a whole city of buildings.

> You can create any kind of game you can imagine with the provided tools

> You can import 3D models or use ones already in Studio

> It is easy to switch to a preview mode to try out your game

WHAT ABOUT THIS CODING STUFF?

This just means adding bits of text ('scripts') to objects so that they behave in certain allocated ways. You'll use scripts from Lua, a Roblox language that was designed to work with C and C++, established programming languages used in everyday software design – but don't worry, it doesn't matter if you've never heard of either of them!

Simply click the + button next to an object, and a space for you to type into will open up: this is called the script tab. Remove any default text that's in there and type your command into it, having consulted a source such as https://devforum.roblox.com first for a list of possible terms. Most of the terms are common – such as 'print' and 'disappear' – but there are some rules to digest, such as the importance of including symbols such as brackets. Do some homework first and you'll be on your way.

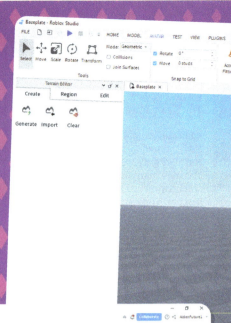

HOW ABOUT THE GAME ENVIRONMENT?

We're glad you asked! Click the Home tab at the top of the screen and then click Editor in the Terrain section. A blue box will pop up and show you where terrain is to be placed, which you can adjust for size and shape.

Once you know where you're dropping your landscape, scroll to the bottom of the Terrain Editor panel and select as many of the features as you wish, such as plains, oceans, sand dunes, mountains, snowscapes, canyons and even lava flows. Use the slider bar below these to adjust the dimensions of the biomes that you're creating, click Generate to create the terrain, and then take a deep breath – this will take your computer a minute to complete!

There's a lot more to say about environment creation, but not enough space here to do it all justice. Dig into the interface and you'll find a suite of terrain-editing tools to rival Photoshop, and the ability to 'paint' your chosen terrain with a very highly customisable 'brush'.

Testing out all the elements of your game before uploading it is very important

HOW DO I TEST MY GAME?

Insert a couple of spawn points with the tool of the same name, go to the Home tab and find a panel with playback controls. Hit the icon with the blue Play triangle: this will load your game and allow you to play your game as an actual Roblox experience. When you're ready to edit again, click the Stop icon (the red square) and you'll be back in edit mode. Don't forget to save as you go along; that button is in the File menu, as you'd expect. You can save a local file to your computer or keep it in the cloud – or both. Give it a cool name that will encourage people to play it: a name like 'Sarah's game in progress version 2.1' probably won't cut it.

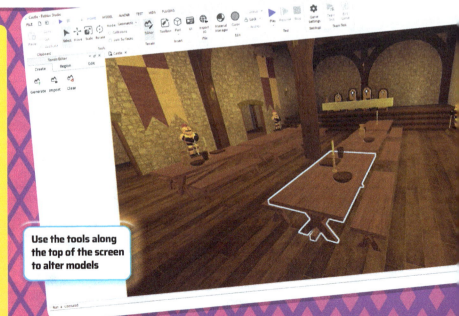

Use the tools along the top of the screen to alter models

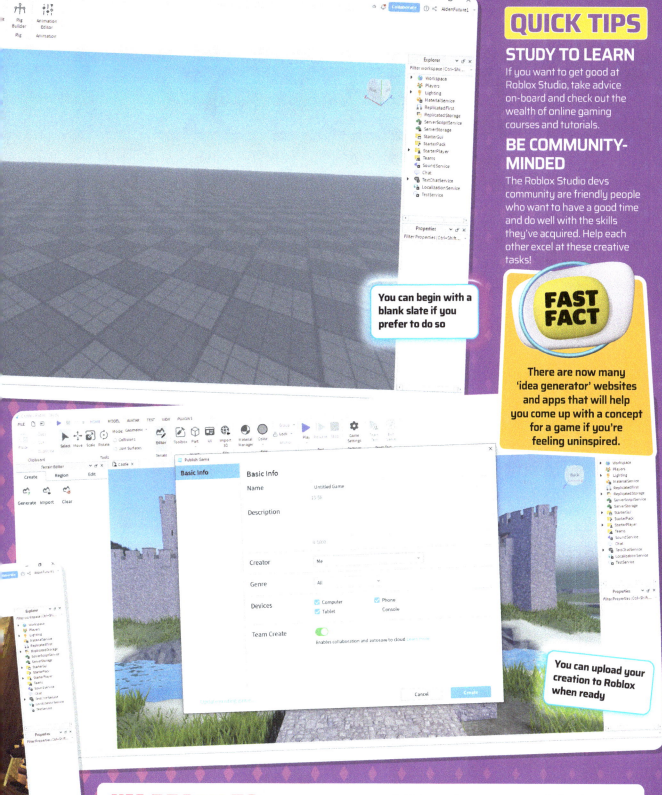

You can begin with a blank slate if you prefer to do so

You can upload your creation to Roblox when ready

I'M READY TO GO PUBLIC!

Great – here's how you publish your game to Roblox. You'll need a Premium Membership to do this. Click File, then Publish To Roblox As, then Create New Game. Add the game name and description, plus creator, genre and compatible console details – and then hit Create. You're out in the open!

If this is your first game, you're unlikely to be greeted with universal praise by its players, but so what? Ignore negative criticism, embrace constructive feedback and treat it as a learning experience. Go back, improve and relaunch your game as Version 2, or use the advice you've been given to create a new and better game. Excellence comes in stages, not all at once, and with enough practice you'll soon be competing at a high level. Good luck!

Future PLC Quay House, The Ambury, Bath, BA1 1UA

Editorial
Group Editor **Dan Peel**
Senior Designer **Adam Markiewicz**
Senior Art Editor **Andy Downes**
Features Editor **Aiden Dalby**
Head of Art & Design **Greg Whitaker**
Editorial Director **Jon White**
Managing Director **Grainne McKenna**

Cover images
Shutterstock, Getty Images

Photography
All copyrights and trademarks are recognised and respected

Advertising
Media packs are available on request
Commercial Director **Clare Dove**

International
Head of Print Licensing **Rachel Shaw**
licensing@futurenet.com
www.futurecontenthub.com

Circulation
Head of Newstrade **Tim Mathers**

Production
Head of Production **Mark Constance**
Production Project Manager **Matthew Eglinton**
Advertising Production Manager **Joanne Crosby**
Digital Editions Controller **Jason Hudson**
Production Managers **Keely Miller, Nola Cokely,
Vivienne Calvert, Fran Twentyman**

Future plc is a public company quoted on the London Stock Exchange (symbol: FUTR)
www.futureplc.com

Chief Executive Officer **Jon Steinberg**
Non-Executive Chairman **Richard Huntingford**
Chief Financial and Strategy Officer **Penny Ladkin-Brand**

Tel +44 (0)1225 442 244

www.ingramcontent.com/pod-product-compliance
Lightning Source LLC
Chambersburg PA
CBHW060157060326
40690CB00018B/4147